BETWEEN GOD AND MAN

BETWEEN GOD AND MAN

A Judgment on War Crimes

A Play in Two Parts
by Kinoshita Junji

Translated, and with an Introduction, by
Eric J. Gangloff

UNIVERSITY OF TOKYO PRESS
UNIVERSITY OF WASHINGTON PRESS
Seattle and London

Translated from the Japanese original
KAMI TO HITO TO NO AIDA (Kōdansha, 1972)

English translation
© 1979 UNIVERSITY OF TOKYO PRESS
Copublished by
University of Tokyo Press and University of Washington Press
ISBN 0-295-95670-4
Library of Congress Catalog Card Number 79-84890
Printed in Japan

Contents

Preface

Kinoshita Junji (1914–) is one of the most prominent modern Japanese dramatists, the author of some forty plays to date. The plays he has written from the time of the Pacific War to the present range over a wide variety of subjects, from historical events to folktales to contemporary events and modern myth-making. He is, moreover, a prolific essayist and theoretician of the drama who has given a strong sense of direction to the modern Japanese theater through the ethical and artistic challenges he has presented to it in his plays and essays.

The present translation introduces Kinoshita's *Kami to hito to no aida* (Between God and Man), first produced in 1970. The translation is based upon the final version of the play, published by Kodansha in Tokyo in 1972.

Kinoshita is known universally in Japan for plays based on old Japanese folktales, which he wrote professionally from the end of the war into the late 1950s. In particular, his folktale play *Yūzuru*[1] (The Twilight Crane) has become a classic of the modern Japanese theater[2] and perhaps even overshadows in reputation the dramatist who wrote it. At the same time Kinoshita has continued to write historical drama from his first play *Fūrō* (Turbulent Waves, 1939) to the present, and it is his historical drama which finally presents the more challenging aspects of his work, in the complexity of its artistry and its thought. In a sense, the folktale theater was an

---

[1]*Yūzuru* has been translated into English by A. C. Scott as *Twilight Crane*, in *Playbook, 5 Plays for a New Theater* (New York: New Directions, 1956).

[2]For detailed histories of the modern Japanese theater the reader is referred to Benito Ortolani's "Fukuda Tsuneari: Modernization and *Shingeki*," in *Tradition and Modernization in Japanese Culture*, ed. by Donald Shively (Princeton: Princeton University Press, 1971) and to J. Thomas Rimer's *Toward a Modern Japanese Theater* (Princeton: Princeton University Press, 1974).

attempt on Kinoshita's part to redefine history, an attempt to reflect the spirit of the Japanese as it is found in folktales rather than to interpret it in orthodox modern Japanese fashion as the resolution of conflicting class interests. The relationship between these two facets of Kinoshita's drama is a complex and fascinating one worthy of a study in its own right. For the purposes of this translation, however, it will suffice to say that Kinoshita has been concerned during his career both with folktales (or, more broadly, with popular forms of literature and theater) and with a generally socialist interpretation of history, primarily of Japanese history.

Kinoshita was born in Tokyo in 1914 and raised and educated there until 1925, when his family moved to the family home in Kumamoto in Kyushu. There he attended Kumamoto Prefectural Middle School and Kumamoto Fifth High School (equivalent to a present-day American college), until in 1936 he returned to Tokyo to enter the Imperial University and study English literature. While working to complete his degree in Elizabethan theater history in the early 1940s, he wrote his early folktale plays. At the end of the war, he began to write professionally, with Yamamoto Yasue as his leading actress, an arrangement that is still current. Kinoshita has helped to promote theater exchanges between Japan and the People's Republic of China, has participated in various societies studying folktales and the Japanese language, and has traveled widely in Europe and Asia. He lives and works in Tokyo at present. Further biographical information can be found in each of the eight volumes of his collected works, *Kinoshita Junji sakuhin shū* (Tokyo: Miraisha, 1962–71) and in the autobiographical sketches in his book *Nihon ga Nihon de aru tame ni wa* (Tokyo: Bungei shunjū shinsha, 1965).

I would like to thank Kinoshita Junji and Yamamoto Yasue for their patient and cordial discussions with me concerning the problems and history of the modern Japanese theater and various problems of style and usage in Mr. Kinoshita's plays. I should also like to express thanks to Edwin McClellan of Yale University for his encouragement in the preparation of this work, and for his many excellent suggestions concerning both the interpretation of the play and the language of its translation. I of course assume all responsibility for the final form of the translation and for any faults it may contain.

I have also received much encouragement and many valuable suggestions in the preparation of the manuscript from friends and colleagues. In particular I would like to thank the members of the Gekidan Mingei troupe in Tokyo for compiling for me a guide to the entries in the historical proceedings of the Tokyo War Crimes Trials, from which parts of the dialogue of the first half of the play were taken. I would also like to thank Michael Povich for his suggestions concerning the use of the more technical language of the first half, and Tsutsumi Masashige and Imaizumi Yoshio for the insights they gave me in the reading of the second half. Much of this work was done at The University of Chicago, and I deeply appreciate the interest in this work taken by my colleagues there. In particular I wish to express thanks to Tetsuo Najita and David Roy for the encouragement they have given me in this work and to Michael Dalby for his comments on the final draft of the manuscript.

I am indebted to The University of Chicago, Division of Humanities, and the Center for Far Eastern Studies of the University for the financial support they have given me in the preparation of this work, and to the Mellon Foundation and Jessie Emmet of the Foundation for the fellowship they provided me in the summer of 1975, which aided me greatly in the completion of the translation. I would also like to thank the staff of University of Tokyo Press, as well as the staff of the Department of Religious Studies, The University of Tennessee, Knoxville, for their generous help in preparing the final manuscript.

Translator's Introduction

I do not like plays to contain pathetic
overtones, they must be convincing like
court pleas. The main thing is to teach
the spectator to reach a verdict.

Bertolt Brecht

. . . we shall change our spectators, who
hitherto have been merely appreciators,
into creators.

Kinoshita Junji

Kinoshita Junji is a didactic dramatist whose didacticism ex-
presses itself as a theory of change: to change the spectator from
appreciator to creator.[1] This seemingly simple formula contains
important implications both for his style of writing and for the focus
of the plays, which ultimately is the audience, not the stage. It is
applied to the members of the audience by heightening their
awareness of contradiction and responsibility; it is applied from
the stage by the presentation of characters who cannot but change
from a lower to a higher level of ethical perception, when they are
faced with the necessity of making personal choices in situations
where all choices lead to destruction in one form or another. Such
internal change by the characters can only be implied on stage; on
the other hand, the actuality of change is the only reasonable explanation for the sudden and drastic acts of Kinoshita's heroes—

[1]Kinoshita Junji, "Shutaiteki ni sōzōteki de aru koto no hitsuyō ni tsuite," in *Nihon
ga Nihon de aru tame ni wa*, p. 270.

1

for example, the hero's use of the young boy as a witness in *Summer: A Romance of the South Seas*, the second half of the present translation. For the most part, Kinoshita presents his characters more as object lessons in ethical behavior than as studies either of personality or of motivation. Clearly, we are meant to see in the behavior of these characters models for conscious, freely determined, ethical acts. Most importantly, we are meant to learn from these models.

Kinoshita often stands close to the surface of his drama. At times it may seem that he preaches; if so, his sermons are not fiery denunciations of political and social inequities of Japanese life, as were those of his predecessors, the socialist dramatists of the early 1930s. Rather, Kinoshita's question is, "How can one be a good Japanese?" and it is posed as enigma and riddle. His drama is one of ideas and form, concerned more with contemporary social issues than with universal truths. It is a strong moral challenge to the audience, written with very carefully constructed dialogue and masterfully created language.

Not surprisingly, then, the drama of Kinoshita is austere and at times heavily political. This is not to say, however, that there are no elements of fantasy or poetry in it. His plays involve a constant inspection of death, guilt, and judgment. These themes are found as subplots, motifs, and underlying fantasy throughout his drama. They are indeed universal issues, but for the most part they are subordinate to the more important issue of the plays, the characters' ethical responses to the situations which evoke these universal themes.[2]

Between God and Man raises the themes of death, guilt, and judgment in the form of two instances of war crimes trials held by the Allies after the Pacific War for crimes allegedly committed by the Japanese. Once again, the main issue of the play is the response of

[2]An interesting comparison can be made between Kinoshita's *Summer: A Romance of the South Seas*, and a 1948 play written by Katō Michio (1918–53), a friend of Kinoshita's in the postwar years. Katō's play is entitled *Jūwa* (Episode) and is subtitled in English by the dramatist *A Tropical Fantasy*. The play is a simple one-act affair, presented as the memories of a narrator who addresses the audience directly from the stage. He tells the story of a division commander stranded on a South Seas island during the war who kills several innocent natives and gradually is made aware of his guilt. The resolution is a form of madness in which the commander remains on the island after the war and prays eternally to the native gods for forgiveness. The most significant element of similarity is perhaps the setting of the stage as a fantasy, a dream play; Katō's uses it for its poetic possibilities, while Kinoshita's elevates the dream element to a metaphysical level in the second half of *Between God and Man*.

each character to the trials. The play is written in two parts, each of which can be produced independently, although ideally the two halves should be produced on alternate nights. The two halves present opposite situations. In the first half, the dramatist presents a case of failure to respond and the consequences of that failure, and in the second half, a fully realized and articulated response and its significance.

The first half is entitled *Shimpan* (The Judgment) and is a realistic recreation of the Tokyo War Crimes Trials held between 1946 and 1948. The play is divided into three acts, set on three separate days in the same courtroom. The characters are the judges, lawyers, and witnesses in the court; the defendants, twenty-eight in all, are seated in the audience, never to appear on stage. The language employed faithfully recreates the highly stylized and technical language of courtroom procedure; a comparison with the proceedings of the historical trials shows that Kinoshita took many of his lines from the proceedings, making, of course, subtle but significant changes in wording, order, and speaker.[3]

The second half is entitled *Natsu: Nampō no romansu* (Summer: A Romance of the South Seas). As the title suggests, the play is a romance, a fantasy, modeled, at least in its language, after the *manzai* stage, a form of popular comedy in modern Japan in which two people, often a woman and a man, the comedienne and her stooge, satirize contemporary issues and personalities in a dialogue in street language, filled with patter and repetition.

The languages of the two parts of Kinoshita's play are strikingly different on the level of diction and articulation. Yet in that neither language bears much resemblance to ordinary conversation, they are strikingly similar, for while the second half is written in a highly colloquial style that gives the illusion of ordinary conversation, it too is formulaic and repetitive, more evocative of the past than informative of the present, concerned with imitating older styles of stage language and with ascertaining the correctness of remembered events. *Summer: A Romance of the South Seas* deals with the war crimes trial of an imaginary private on a name-

---

[3]A record of the proceedings in Japanese, upon which Kinoshita presumably relied, is found in *Kyokutō kokusai gunji saiban sokkiroku*, 10 v., ed. by Nitta Mitsuo (Tokyo: Yūshōdō, 1968). For the translation I have relied on *International Military Tribunal for the Far East: Proceedings 1946–1948* (microfilm, undated).

less South Seas island. The play, in four acts, divides its time between the courtroom on the island directly after the war and a small neighborhood park in Tokyo, sometime in the mid-1950s. In essence both halves deal with the act and art of self-judgment, the first half by obvious silence, the second by active demonstration.

The Judgment

The first act of *The Judgment* concentrates on the question of the jurisdiction of the court; the second, on the credibility of the evidence presented by the prosecution; the third, on the definition of the term "war crime." Act I is taken mainly from the records of May 4, 6, 13, and 17, 1946, during the actual proceedings; Act II from January 16 and 17, 1947; Act III from March 3 and 5, 1947.

The judges and attorneys who appear on stage are there as functionaries of the court. Their personal thoughts and idiosyncracies are stifled by the court roles they don, and particularly by the language they speak while in court, a highly repetitive, sonorous, and formal speech. At certain times, there are hints of personality in the language, as in the speeches of the Chief Counsel of Act I, whose ideas are expressed in such old-fashioned, formal circumlocutions that he appears out of place in the court. For the most part, however, the language is confined to the jargon and clichés of the courtroom. In effect, the court is allowed to speak for itself on the stage.

The audience may come to the play expecting a traditional courtroom melodrama, but if it does, it will soon be disappointed, for the "arguments" of the first act are purely formal questions. Even before the arraignment of the defendants begins, the defense complains:

> Let us set aside for the moment the fact that this court is being carried out in the language and customs of the Anglo-American legal system. From the point of view of the continental legal system, which Japan has followed up to now, is it not a fact that the President of the tribunal has combined in his person both judge and prosecutor? That is

impermissible under any rule of modern law. It is a contradiction. Why does the President violate this legal principle?

The objection points out a fundamental, if not *the* fundamental, problem of the court. The President, however, dismisses it and proceeds with the arraignment. Each defendant pleads not guilty, and the play begins.

The first act is then spent arguing whether the court actually has jurisdiction over the defendants. The latter are charged on fifty-five counts of crimes against peace, murder and conventional war crimes, and crimes against humanity. The prosecution bases its right to bring these charges on the various declarations and proclamations it presents after the arraignment, but a much more immediate claim is implied:

> The proponents of these motions [to deny the court jurisdiction] claim that these leaders, directors, and officials, having obtained the power to bring this ruin and destruction about—having planned, prepared, and initiated it—can never be brought to the bar of justice. The necessary corollary follows that the helpless dupes and victims who were subject to their control and orders, as well as the millions of other innocent victims, will undergo forever the untold suffering these acts brought upon them, while these leaders remain free from punishment.

The prosecution claims an eye for an eye—that is, the justice of the victor. The defense argues that before the signing of the Instrument of Surrender, "crimes against peace" and "crimes against humanity" were unknown and so cannot be used to indict the defendants. The argument appears to be a mere technicality, as the prosecution claims, but without such "mere technicalities" a court can be used as an instrument to perpetrate injustice, as we begin to suspect this court will be used. For at the end of the act, the President denies the defense motion and refuses to give his reasons for denying it.

The second act opens along the lines of the prosecution's logic: What has been done is obvious and must be punished in some way, regardless of formal questions. The wronged must be recompensed, and the future security of the world must be assured. During the act, the President of the tribunal, who so far has appeared only as the ostensible referee, gives the full support of the court to this logic:

> It is necessary for every person in this court, and for all people in the world, to call to mind at every instant the mission of this international tribunal. We are here to make clear to the world war crimes against humanity.

The prosecution brings forth the French witness, who adds details to the documentation of atrocities committed by the Japanese in Indo-China. Step by step, the defense undermines the witness's credibility. The defense never argues that the dead Frenchmen had not been tortured and killed by the Japanese. It merely forces the admission from the witness that the dead were probably Free French guerrillas and that the witness himself was Vichy French. The fact that the murdered men were guerrillas and not prisoners of war means that their murder cannot be considered an atrocity under international law. They may well have been killed by Japanese, but that fact has nothing to do with the twenty-eight defendants in this court. The court itself is not eager to recognize this position, and the act ends unresolved. The court may or may not reject the evidence of atrocities committed by Japanese military forces submitted thus far by the prosecution.

The third act opens with the theme of guilt: How is the guilt of an entire nation to be defined at times of war? The prosecution apparently is basing its accusation against the twenty-eight defendants on various treaties, particularly the Kellogg-Briand Peace Pact, for the defense is attacking the validity of these treaties with great vigor. The defense argues that all the major powers had broken these treaties prior to the war, and thereby either had invalidated the treaties or else are equally guilty of war crimes. The prosecution answers that only one case is being tried, the case of Japan. Is Japan guilty of war crimes or not? Prosecuting Attorney B, an Englishman, reminds the defense that its logic would ultimately bring America to the stand for having dropped the atomic bomb. Defense Attorney F, an American, falters and answers that he has no desire to "investigate" any of the breaches, including those by the Japanese. He merely wishes the court to be aware of these other breaches. He thus recognizes the carefully maintained balance of truth and convenience that all members of the court struggle to maintain.

Nationality has so far played no part in the proceedings. With the introduction of the topic of the bomb, however, the nationalities of the various members of the court begin to force the members out of their strictly defined court roles. Defense Attorney G, an American, begins to act peculiar once the bomb is mentioned and is thereby made an identifiable "American." The Russian Prosecuting Attorney C becomes identifiable by his political maneuvering, when he accuses the Americans of sophistry. The introduction of national causes makes the play of attack and defense increasingly difficult, for the court members must now act both as officers of a supposedly impartial court and as defenders of their national causes.

The right to judge rests on the facade of legitimacy that the court has maintained so far, and if that facade is torn away, the court will have no right to exist. The play now has a certain tension to it, for all the participating members, particularly the Americans, must proceed without implicating their own countries in the charges. The judges rule that the defense may offer its documentation of breaches of treaties on the part of the major powers for the court record, but that it will not be admitted as evidence. The submission begins in a long, slow, and surprisingly perfunctory manner. At one point, the English prosecuting attorney uses a document of the defense as proof of a general conspiracy by the Japanese against world peace. The victory is small; the defense ignores this minor defeat and quickly ends the submission. Obviously, the defense is as interested in minimizing the significance of these documents as in using them for support. The court is already compromised.

In the next speech, an American, Defense Attorney G, upsets the balance between truth and expediency and forces the court to show its arbitrary nature. His action is a purely personal gesture; his speech satirizes the tactics of expediency taken by his colleague F as he openly accuses America of having committed a war crime by dropping the bomb. The President breaks in, and G accuses him of interfering with the defense's right to speak. G in turn is charged with contempt of court. The order of the court and the control of the court over its contradictory elements are gone; chaos reigns as various members rise to promote national causes, and the court calls a recess to preserve a semblance of order. The guilt of Japan becomes irrelevant to the proceedings.

After the recess, the court dismisses G for contempt. The court has now become a cause unto itself, interested in its own preservation and, by implication, the preservation of the victor's right to punish the vanquished. The semblance of legitimacy has been stripped from it completely. In Act I, the jurisdiction of the court, and in Act II, the evidence of the prosecution were questioned by the defense; the court managed to avoid the questions. In Act III, the questions almost destroy the court, and the court responds by arbitrarily judging its own members. The court as a place where the trial of the Japanese can be held objectively has disappeared. Instead of being judged, the Japanese are merely being sentenced.

One must keep in mind that throughout the play, the contradictions of the court are pointed out by the American attorneys for the defense, for it is the only means they have of providing a fair defense in what is essentially a kangaroo court. The American attorneys for the defense were placed in a difficult situation in the historical trials for the same reason: they had to ignore the interests of their own country in order to work effectively. The courage with which they faced this unwelcome task has been mentioned by Japanese commentators on the trials[4] and is shown convincingly by Kinoshita in the figures of E in Act II and G in Act III. Yet even these two seem pale as heroic figures, and one realizes once again that Kinoshita is not interested in the actual people who participated in the trials so much as in certain ethical problems of those trials.

A trial, it seems, is like a play. As Hannah Arendt observes:

> A trial resembles a play in that both begin and end with the doer, not with the victim. A show trial needs even more urgently than an ordinary trial a limited and well-defined outline of what was done and how it was done. In the center of a trial can only be the one who did—in this respect, he

[4]Miyashita Nobuo, "Tōkyō saiban to *Shimpan*," *Higeki kigeki* (February, 1971), pp. 61–66.

is like the hero in the play—and if he suffers, he must suffer
for what he has done, not for what he has caused others to
suffer.[5]

Yet in this play there are no defendants—they are seated in the
audience. The only characters present are the judges, the prosecuting attorneys, and the defending attorneys, who are presented
respectively as bullies, tricksters, and compromised men. The play
as such draws a negative portrait of the Tokyo Trials and can be
taken on one level as an indictment of those trials, but it is far too
dispassionate, in both language and action, to be taken merely as
a statement of outrage.

In the end, Defense Attorney H, the only Japanese present, asks
the court to remember those who died in Hiroshima and Nagasaki,
and the President dismisses him thus: "Your feelings have no relevance to this court." Both parties are justified in their responses,
but both have missed the point. The problem is that this court
offered no possibility to the Japanese for the self-examination that
ought to accompany a trial of this magnitude. Because the court
dealt with the matter in terms of expediency, the twenty-eight may
well have been punished, but the original question of the guilt of
these men—and, more broadly, of the nation—has never been
resolved, and it is with this latter question that the play is finally
involved.

In Kinoshita's handling of the Tokyo War Crimes Trials, the
defendants are effaced from the play, which their existence has
brought into being, and we can only wonder finally what he thinks
of them. Presumably he does not exonerate them from responsibility or moral culpability simply because the trials were biased,
yet this is not made clear in *The Judgment*. In fact, the only thing
clear is that the question of culpability never becomes a problem for
the trial.

In *The Judgment* Kinoshita works on several levels, which are
presented in an order of increasing significance and of increasing
abstraction. There is the issue of the biases of the historical trials
and of the various persons involved in the trials—the judges and
attorneys. There is also the issue of personal responsibility involved

[5]Hannah Arendt, *Eichmann in Jerusalem* (New York: Viking Press, 1964), p. 9.

in these trials. On the most concrete level, Kinoshita presents the responses of Attorneys E and G to the trial on stage as models of behavior. However, on the level that we might legitimately expect the dramatist to concentrate on, the level of the responses of the twenty-eight defendants, he is silent. The defendants never are allowed to defend themselves, and we never know what their thoughts are. On the one hand, this argument by silence may be the only reasonable response they could have made to a biased court. On the other hand, however biased this court may be, clearly it presents an opportunity to establish the origins of the Pacific War and of the destruction it caused, and no one takes advantage of this opportunity in the play. In this sense, the responses of the defendants to the trial on stage can be taken only as an evasion, or as an anti-model of behavior, and we are led to ask what their responses during the historical trials were. Yet the play does not touch upon this point. In *The Judgment*, it seems, Kinoshita is interested even more in moving his audience to a sense of dissatisfaction through his presentation of the trials than in exploring the personal responsibility of any of the defendants. He is interested in moving his audience to ask who the rightful defendants of this trial were and what a proper response to the trials by those rightful defendants might have been at the time of the Tokyo Trials.

Kinoshita seeks to involve his audience in the play in an active, personal way. On this level, the highest level, he works at creating an audience of "creators." His aim is to "grasp history" through drama, as he has often phrased it[6]—or, to use the symbolists' terms, to bring into consciousness forgotten fears, anxieties, guilt, and dread in order to make his audience deal with them on a conscious, public level.[7] *The Judgment* deals with twenty-five years of time from the Tokyo Trials to the production of the play. These years are not a span of time but a vacuum in time, in which the facts of war—the atrocities and bombings—have been relegated to oblivion by the Japanese. These forgotten facts, rather than legal

---

[6]For Kinoshita's most comprehensive statement of his view of dramaturgy as historiography, see "*Makubesu* shiron: Rekishi to iū mono," in his book *Dorama no sekai* (Tokyo: Miraisha, 1967). See also, for example, his discussion of the phrase in "Gendaigeki no fukkatsu," in *Shin Nihon bungaku* (July, 1956), pp. 86–100.

[7]Hugh Duncan, *Symbols in Society* (New York: Oxford University Press, 1968), pp. 125–26.

definition, seem to constitute both the history and the guilt in the play, terms which can be used practically synonymously. Kinoshita wisely chooses not to bring these aspects out onto the stage itself, but only to suggest the ways in which they have been kept from sight by the audience—a Japanese audience.

How does this come about? How will the audience participate in the play? How does the play become a living metaphor? It has been argued effectively that the twenty-eight, public officials in Japan during the war, were functioning only in constitutional modes and under the pressure of public opinion.[8] This argument seems to be an assumption in Kinoshita's play as well, for if it is true, then the constitution—or, more appropriately, the public opinion that supported this constitution—was the rightful object of the trial, an idea which has received little, if any, public support. The play is written in such a way that the members of the audience will recognize the responsibility that has existed hidden and unexamined within themselves since the war. The play is successful not because it "dramatizes" the Tokyo Trials and gives the original record exciting and unexpected twists; it is successful because it recreates the trials and involves the audience in the trial process, something the original trials failed to do, from Kinoshita's point of view.

In the end, the Japanese Attorney H steps forth to protest the callous use of the atomic bomb. His protest is surprisingly weak, and the entire court turns on him. Like Defense Attorney H, the Japanese audience has been excluded from the court. Like the defendants, it can only watch the court in silence. The court is a kangaroo court, but that is not the final reason why the Japanese have been excluded from it. They have been excluded because they have refused to commit themselves to any such trial and, like H, have gnashed their teeth in righteous indignation over the injuries they have received. They have refused to stand up and make a place for themselves in this trial and have let the twenty-eight be sentenced instead, only to turn around afterward and call the trials a formalized tragedy of revenge (as Japanese commentators have in fact done).[9]

If the play is successful, the audience will be struck by the sight

---

[8]R. B. Pal, *International Military Tribunal for the Far East: Dissentient Judgment of Justice Pal* (Calcutta: Sanyal & Company, 1953), p. 698 ff.

[9]Miyashita, "Tōkyō saiban," p. 66.

of the twenty-eight seated in the audience: The guilty are among us; the guilty are none other than us; we have no place to take this burden and lay it bare except within ourselves. The failure of the court, which has occupied the action of the play, is transcended in this metaphor. Values are reversed. To judge oneself, most likely to judge oneself guilty, becomes a positive act, for it signifies that the spectator has found the strength to push himself that far. The play ends with this judgment.

Summer: A Romance of the South Seas

Summer: A Romance of the South Seas attempts to formulate the question of where guilt lies in a positive, even affirmative, manner. In this second half, the hero (for there is a hero on stage this time), a man formally innocent of charges brought against him which have led to his death sentence, discovers that the guilt for those crimes does lie finally within himself. The play recounts the process by which he learns to accept and to value the discovery.

Some ten years after the war, Kanohara, formerly a private superior first-class (a rank in the Imperial Army between private first-class and corporal), waits in prison in the South Pacific to be executed. He and the other soldiers of his brigade, who had been stationed with him on a small island, were tried directly after the war for war crimes committed against the natives of the island. Although he and many others were convicted and condemned to death, in many cases the sentences still have not been carried out.

On the day depicted in the play, a group of his friends and relatives in Tokyo gather by chance. The group includes his wife Kiyoko and his young son, three soldiers who had served with him and returned safely to Tokyo, and Tobosuke, a comedienne from the *manzai* stage with whom Kanohara had had an affair before marrying his wife.

The three soldiers had served time in prison for war crimes, and now, once again free, they feel it their responsibility to inquire after the fate of the men still in prison and to pay occasional visits to the families of these men. By the time the play opens, it seems that both the visits and the families' responses have become mechanical; the past, in fact, has become buried beneath the very rituals instituted to keep its memory alive. Only Tobosuke is aware of this, and it becomes her purpose in the play to explode these rituals and to reinvest the past, now half-alive, half-dead in prison and in memory, with the vitality she believes it deserves. On the day of the play, through the meeting of this group, she sets about to discover how this act of "retrieving the irretrievable" can be accomplished.

With the coming of the war and Kanohara's marriage, the relationship between Tobosuke and Kanohara had been broken off, but they apparently continued to love each other, for on the night before he was to be drafted, he visited her in her theater and later walked with her to a small park near his home, where the two sat and talked through the night. The memory of their relationship obsesses Tobosuke. She has spent the years since the war steeped in her memories, unresponsive to the world, waiting for news either of Kanohara's release or of his execution. At one point, she recites lines from "The Judge from the South Seas," a romantic ballad performed once by chanters in the silent movie houses, as a private tribute to the love she shared with him. Several times she repeats one of the ballad's lines, "A spray of stars across the purple twilight sky," to evoke the world of past love. She would like to be free, to forget everything completely, but she cannot. She is tainted with death; she would prefer to have Kanohara die, and therefore be always free, than have him return as Kiyoko's husband. She remains faithful to the memory of the man, not only because of her love but also because of the intimate acquaintance she has with the power his death holds.

Man A, one of Kanohara's army buddies, had delivered a letter from Kanohara to Tobosuke on his return to Tokyo, and an acquaintance developed between them. Today, when Tobosuke has come to the park again to brood, Man A passes by on his way to visit Kanohara's wife. They meet and begin a conversation. As the dialogue proceeds in good *manzai* fashion, Man A makes a tentative overture to a declaration of love. Tobosuke is the means by which he hopes to start life anew. Tobosuke speaks of past love as a warning when she recites the lines of the ballad, but Man A, oblivious to her meaning, proceeds to express his sentiments more forcefully.

Tobosuke toys with the hints of love he so haplessly offers and banters with the man, but she will not take him seriously, for while he truly desires to forget the past, she is ambivalent. More than that, however, she is contemptuous of his belief that what happened in the trials was merely a stroke of bad luck that cannot be construed to have meaning. For his belief would ultimately reduce Kanohara's life and imminent death to the level of triviality, a state she cannot accept.

By the end of the act, the two other army friends, Man B and Man C, have gathered in the park to set out together to visit Kanohara's wife. Before they leave, in the course of their conversation, Tobosuke believes she overhears the news that notification of the execution has finally arrived. In a state of shock, she sets out with the three men to meet with Kiyoko, planning to divulge the secret of her former affair with Kanohara.

By the opening of Act II, Tobosuke has already revealed the details of the affair and now nervously waits for Kiyoko's angry reaction. In this scene again two people appear on stage alone, speaking dialogue in *manzai* fashion, but Tobosuke is no longer the obvious superior. Kiyoko is an "intellectual," a woman of refinement and education, who easily carries her own against Tobosuke's sallies. Her tactic is to remain irritatingly calm. She asks of Tobosuke only one thing, to explain to her why she gratuitously revealed her secret. Tobosuke is confused, but the question intrigues her and draws from her a certain respect for the wife. Kiyoko too, it seems, is willing to fight for the memory of her husband, but this soon proves to be an illusion: Kiyoko speaks of the shame of being the wife of a war criminal whose guilt has been proved by God Himself. It occurs to Tobosuke that she is different from Kiyoko, for she cannot simply give up and accept these events as some incomprehensible act of God. She must find something to do—not merely circulating petitions for clemency, as Kiyoko has done: now that he is dead she must find a way to transform the banal reality of the trials and executions. This is what she apparently would tell Kiyoko if she could find the words, but instead she can only tell her the news of the execution and about her desire to defy God's judgment of Kanohara, if that is what it is.

A new question arises in the conversation between the two women: If both Man A and Kanohara performed the same duties in the army from the time they were inducted, why was Man A able to return alive when Kanohara was executed? Men A, B, and C soon meet with the women, who confront them with the question. There is, of course, no way for them to answer except by recounting the particular circumstances of the trial, and thus we are taken into Act III, the heart of the play, a flashback to the last days of the war on the island and the trials which followed.

In the last days before the defeat, a fear of spy rings had swept through the Japanese command. The order to exterminate any islander suspected of spy activities was passed down through the ranks to the bottom, to Kanohara and his friends. Several tribunals were held in which a great number of islanders, presumably innocent, were found guilty and executed. In addition, two people, an old man and a woman, died in the course of interrogation, the woman having committed suicide to escape torture.

Act III is constructed of scenes of three kinds: scenes of interrogation and torture before the defeat; scenes of the soldiers in prison waiting for the trial; scenes of the trial. They are tacked on one after another in the fashion of a person's attempting to puzzle out some significant pattern from a collection of random and fragmentary memories. The overall impression one receives from the act is that of a dream remembered long after awakening. In the course of the flashback, it is made clear that in the army sheer arbitrariness reigned. Orders from a superior could not be questioned, and the commanding officers on the island were either ruthless or spineless. It is also made clear that while Kanohara was present at the interrogation of the woman, he opposed torturing her at great risk to his own safety, while Man A eagerly participated in the act to avoid jeopardizing himself. Yet Kanohara was executed for this very affair, while Man A was set free. Tobosuke demands to know why, but the men have no answer. The answer to her question lies in the moment Kanohara is accused as a guilty party by the woman's son, and the fragments are assembled to provide an increasingly complex and comprehensive picture of the events leading up to that moment.

In this second play, the lessons concerning courtroom justice, so carefully prepared in *The Judgment*, are assumed without comment. The court is a parody of the Tokyo tribunal, the members of the court cast as monkeys sitting in tree branches, chattering

instead of talking. The pompous rhetoric of the prosecutor in
The Judgment here is reduced to mere verbiage. No case is given
more than a few minutes, and men are condemned to death simply
because a file may have been numbered incorrectly. The only
thing necessary for the court is that there be a sufficient number
of convictions.

As the soldiers wait in prison for their turns to appear in court,
Kanohara watches the men in adjoining cells frantically attempting to plan some strategy for the courtroom. He has written a
brief poem about life in this prison:

> Someone's going to die, and it's either me or you.
> Don't worry, brother, it's my turn to walk the rope.
> Left, right, step by step—it's a dangerous game we play.
> Fall with a thump and you're off to hell—step by step.

He has written this in the guise of a man walking a tightrope;
the poem is written on a wall as the graffiti of a man waiting to
be hanged. He sees the arbitrary nature of the trials clearly and
understands that only a few will survive and will do so at the
expense of the others. Suicide is a possible answer, which he first
rejects, preferring to hold out and fight. But the problem of his
own guilt occupies more and more of his attention, as is evident
in the following scene:

KANOHARA   Well, the truth is, I was thinking about the problem
of guilt.

MAN A   Guilt? Guilt? What's the problem? They brought us in
because we're guilty, didn't they?

KANOHARA   Don't be a fool! No one goes around calling himself
guilty. That's the problem with the Japanese, we all agree
with the man on top. There's something cheap about that.

MAN A   You mean the Allies must have done things as bad as we
did?

KANOHARA   Which means our lots are really the same, only
they've convinced themselves they're God right now.

MAN A   I see.

KANOHARA   But if we had won, we'd have done the same, I'm
sure.

MAN A   We would?
KANOHARA   That is where guilt lies.

This scene marks the first time Kanohara faces "guilt" in a personal way. What the nature of that guilt is is not made clear. We cannot know much about it other than that it underlies his rejection of the relativity he finds in victory, whether on the battlefield or in court. From subsequent events and statements in the play, we are led to believe that from this moment on Kanohara seeks some means of breaking through this relativity, so that he might confront this guilt he has perceived on a purely subjective level as an impersonal, objective reality.

Kanohara searches back in his memory to the time when the woman under interrogation committed suicide, for in the ongoing trial this particular incident has become a major concern. And although he can find no evidence of conscious intention to torture, neither can he find any proof that he acted positively to prevent harm. In his mind, then, he makes that positive act and declares himself guilty. At the end of the act, he contrives to have the young son of the tortured woman, a boy too young to understand the meaning of what he does, called into court as a witness. In the courtroom, the boy points at Kanohara as a party to his mother's death. The court declares him guilty.

The scene of the trial and the island are in fact the memories of Man A played out on stage, and in the last act the group is released from its reverie. The work of piecing together the man's memories of Kanohara, the war, and the trial through Tobosuke's medium is completed; her work of defying God is finished—the work of retrieving what of significance lay buried in the past. The significance of Kanohara's death was not that it was an outrageous example of a miscarriage of legal justice—which indeed it was—but that Kanohara chose death as a means of pushing himself beyond the randomness and relativity of both the army and the court to a prior principle he called "guilt."[10]

The group comes back to its senses when its dream has finally

[10]The first essay of significant length to be written in Japanese on Kinoshita's drama, "Kinoshita Junji no dorama ni okeru genzai ishiki," has been published by Takeda Kiyoko in her book *Haikyōsha no keifu* (Tokyo: Iwanami, 1973). She begins her study with Kinoshita's conversion to Christianity in his Kumamoto days and later "aposta-

been pieced together, but only Tobosuke awakes with an answer to the riddle it poses: The dream was of God, of justice obtainable some place other than on earth; but God is only the name of the impersonal force of history, an unutterable chaos culminating in death. If justice is to be obtained, it can come only from within. The significance of Kanohara's act of calling in the boy as a witness was that he had the courage to pursue justice, even at the cost of his life. God never existed; only history, an accumulation of past evils, grinding on to frustrate man's will, remains.

All that remains for Tobosuke is to make peace with her memories; for Kiyoko and the men, the process of committing those memories once again to oblivion begins immediately. The three men reject them as nothing more than a bad dream, while Kiyoko, who understands their significance, insists on relegating them to a state of never having been, knowing full well that she can never do so completely. Only Tobosuke insists that they remain in active memory as a memorial to a man who did what he thought was right.

When all the others have left, Tobosuke once again meets with Kanohara in reverie and promises to erect his tombstone in her heart, to stand as a memorial to his act. Oblivion is the wisdom of Kiyoko and the men, for it allows them to live free of the past;

---

sy" (Kinoshita's word, according to Takeda, but unfortunately no reference is given) and then identifies the sense of guilt in his drama as Christian original sin, or a residual element of it, transformed into a more traditional Japanese perspective. This conclusion, and the further conclusion she draws that Kinoshita's sense of history is something very close to a Christian sense of God, differ from those in this essay in their denial of the basic historicity of the guilt Kinoshita wishes to illuminate.

It is in fact tempting to see Christian messages in Kinoshita's plays, as, for example, in Kanohara's death. Was it actually suicide? Did he mean it to be an act of self-sacrifice by which he could redeem the lives of other soldiers and atone for the guilt of the world by imitating Christ? There is significant evidence to suggest it is, and there is equally significant evidence to suggest it is not; in fact, Kanohara denies it outright. The dramatist remains ambiguous on this point, if not ambivalent, and if he is consciously working with Christian theology, he is eager to deny it. On the other hand, the significance of Kanohara's act as an ethical response to a set of pressing, immediate circumstances and, more abstractly, as a means of confronting the objective reality of history is much clearer. These lead us far from a Christian message and cannot be overlooked.

Takeda's essay is nonetheless extremely interesting as an example of an attempt to assay prior motivation (if we choose to ignore the dramatist's consciously didactic purpose) in Kinoshita's drama, whether that be of the characters (did Kanohara intend to die or merely to create the ultimate game of chance?) or of the dramatist, in seeking influences on his work. The essay is a stimulating contribution in its interpretation of ultimate influence.

but it means they may repeat and allow to be repeated the mistakes of the past. Tobosuke, to serve as witness to the evils of the past, is left with her heart entombed in memory, half-alive, half-dead, a medium between two worlds with the power to speak with the wisdom of the dead, and the victim of the power of their guilt.

Kinoshita Junji writes specifically for a Japanese audience. His plays deal with issues in Japanese history and are written to lead the audience to draw conclusions about these issues. In *Between God and Man* he first inspects the Tokyo War Crimes Trials and presents them in such a way that the audience will conclude that the historical trials held no possibility of reaching an impartial decision about any of the twenty-eight defendants. As a further conclusion, the audience is asked not to react in self-righteous and impotent indignation, but to consider its place, member by member, in the history that led to those trials and to consider the possibility that the responsibility for that history might very well have lain, and may still lie, within each of them, and not merely within the twenty-eight.

Then, in the second half of the play, the dramatist presents a character who entertains personally responsibility and guilt for crimes that no one else would atone for. A lowly private is forced to stand trial for war crimes and in the process realizes that each person, beginning with himself, must accept guilt, regardless of formal innocence or court decisions. Knowledge implies action for Kinoshita, for once a person acquires such knowledge, he is responsible to act on it. Consequently, the private manipulates the random nature of the court decisions, allows a boy too young to know what he is doing to choose the guilty parties, and is finally chosen himself.

Summer: A Romance of the South Seas is about two people, Kanohara and Tobosuke, whose natures lead them invariably to question the meaning of their acts. Tobosuke the comedienne makes a comedy of this in Act I when she questions the significance of questioning. She resolves the problem by pursuing the act of questioning rather than contemplating the form of the question, the terms she will frame it in. Pursuit, positive action, the desire to resolve contradictions rather than to contemplate them are

important characteristics of the intellectual; the comedy of
Tobosuke's intense pursuit foreshadows the tragedy of Kanohara's.

For Tobosuke, the true intellectual is a man like Kanohara, a
man whose principles lead him from thought to action in order
that he might set an example. In her words:

> He took it upon himself to play a dangerous game. Left,
> right, step by step—it's a dangerous game we play. He
> didn't play it like some of the others did, trying to find a
> way out. He took it on and staked his very life on that game.
> He did it to protect what was most important to him.

The sad part is that no matter how many examples there may be,
the world will forget them, and so the process of setting examples
must go on indefinitely. In the end, in answer to both halves of
the play, a woman enshrines her heart to the memory of the
private and becomes one more willing victim of the war.

The two halves of *Between God and Man* offer an interesting
contrast in their presentations of history,[11] just as they do in the
use of language. *The Judgment* presents the record, a concrete,
objective artifact, which becomes meaningful history only when it
is interpreted; and, as the play so clearly implies, to interpret
is to apply values, to judge. On the surface the play preserves the
facade of the historical monument, drawn as it is in crisp, clear
lines, like a rubbing of a gravestone. *Summer: A Romance of the
South Seas* presents history as subjective memory. The characters
are literally "lost in memory," whether that state be reverie,
oblivion, or Tobosuke's enshrinement at the end of the play. The
play deals not so much with the application of values as with
the creation of values from experience. History here is something
which is made by man, literally created by the mind, and which
can be changed by man. And if the experiences from which one
creates values are in the past, then one must go back to them—
"retrieve the irretrievable," says Tobosuke—and remake one's
mind, regardless of the cost.

[11]For an earlier essay on Kinoshita's historiography, see Mori Arimasa, "Le Dra-
maturge Japonais: Kinoshita Junji," in *Les Théâtres d'Asie*, ed. by Jean Jacquot (Paris:
Centre National de la Recherche Scientifique, 1961).

It is significant that this play and many others in Kinoshita's output concern the Pacific War. Kinoshita belongs to a tradition of historical dramatists stretching back through the prewar socialist dramatists to the very first dramatists of the modern Japanese theater. Each generation involved in this tradition has written history according to its own experience, and for Kinoshita and his generation, that experience has been defined to a great degree by the war. It is therefore fitting that his drama should be to a great extent an interpretation of that war, a memorial to the world destroyed by it, a requiem for those who died in it, and, above all, a reminder to those who survived it of the price each person must pay for survival.

A scene from "The Judgment," performed at Sabō Kaikan Hall, Tokyo, November 1970. Takizawa Osamu as the Chief Prosector. Courtesy of Gekidan Mingei.

A scene from "The Judgment," performed at Sabō Kaikan Hall, Tokyo, November 1970. Ōtaki Shūji as Chief Counsel for the Defense at the speaker's stand. Courtesy of Gekidan Mingei.

BETWEEN GOD AND MAN

Part I   The Judgment

It would be difficult to explain the relationship between the historical facts and the fiction which are mixed together in this work. The stage layout and setting may be treated realistically or abstractly; the exact shading between these two will depend on the director's understanding of the relationship between historical fact and fiction in the play.

The following words are to be projected on a screen to the rear of the stage for a short while before the house lights are dimmed:

ALL RESEMBLANCES BETWEEN ACTUAL EVENTS AND PEOPLE AND THOSE FOUND IN THIS PLAY ARE INTENTIONAL

The following words are to be projected on the screen after the house lights are dimmed and are to remain on the screen until the end of the play:

INTERNATIONAL MILITARY TRIBUNAL FAR EAST —TOKYO

Act I

CHARACTERS

Judge A (New Zealander)
Chief Counsel for the Defense (Japanese)
Chief Prosecutor (American)
President of the Tribunal (Australian)
Defense Attorney A (American)
Defense Attorney B (American)
Marshal of the Court (American)

Language Monitor (probably a second-generation Japanese-American heard only as a voice)
A-Class Defendants, except Ōkawa Shūmei (they are seated in the audience)

JUDGE A   [*His face is suddenly illuminated on the dark stage. His position is high, stage center; it will be determined by the construction of the courtroom. Solemnly*]   The International Military Tribunal for the Far East was convened three days ago with all due solemnity by the opening address of the President. The first document to be read was the long indictment, consisting of fifty-five charges against the twenty-eight defendants. Immediately following this, we proceeded to the arraignment, in which each defendant was to be asked to plead guilty or not guilty to the charges. At that point, however, two incidents suddenly prevented a prompt dispatching of the procedure.

One was an unexpected incident. The head of the accused Ōkawa Shūmei was suddenly hit from behind by the accused Tōjō Hideki.

MONITOR   [*mechanically*]   Correction by the language monitor. The head of Tōjō Hideki was suddenly hit from behind by Ōkawa Shūmei. It was hit with a loud slap.

JUDGE A   By motion of his counsel, Ōkawa Shūmei was removed from the dock and placed under the observation of three psychiatrists, who will determine whether or not he is mentally competent.

Second, a challenge was suddenly raised today by the Chief Counsel for the Defense against the President of the tribunal. The court has just now taken a fifteen-minute recess, during which time the members of the tribunal, in the absence of the President, conferred upon this challenge. The members have asked me, who presided at their conference, to make the announcement of their decision to the members of this court. Our decision—

CHIEF COUNSEL   [*His face is suddenly illuminated. His position is low, stage center.*]   Before the decision is stated, I would like permission to make a statement as Chief Counsel.

His Honor, the President, declared this recess in a great hurry, almost in a rage, before I had sufficient time to state the reasons for my challenge. I have not raised this challenge against His Honor the President alone. I wish to make the motion against each of the members of the tribunal. To raise an objection does not mean that I have any lack of respect for this court. I venture to do this in order that the historical mission of this court may truly be accomplished. I would expect His Honor, as President of the tribunal, to declare a recess only after having listened to all my reasons in full.

CHIEF PROSECUTOR [*His face is suddenly illuminated next to that of the Chief Counsel. He speaks indignantly, as if to push the Chief Counsel away from the microphone.*] I speak as Chief Prosecutor on behalf of the prosecution. If the defense has any objections to this International Military Tribunal for the Far East, it should submit them in the form of a written motion in compliance with the rules of the "Charter of the International Military Tribunal for the Far East."

CHIEF COUNSEL I am challenging the judges of this tribunal. This challenge, this recusation is neither a motion nor an application which is "to be submitted in written form" as provided for in the regulations of Article 10 of the Charter which you speak of.

CHIEF PROSECUTOR However, Article 10, you will remember, provides that "motions, applications, and other requests made against the court are to be submitted in written form." Consequently, challenges as well—

CHIEF COUNSEL I do not think that a challenge against a judge is included under the provisions of Article 10. My reason is that it arises from the exigencies of the courtroom.

CHIEF PROSECUTOR I shall not enter into the question of whether the challenge against the President suggested itself spontaneously to you as you were looking at him today. It is important that you remember one fact: We are arguing in a court which has been established by the "Special Proclamation—Establishment of an International Military Tribunal for the Far East" and its appendix, the "Charter of the International Military Tribunal for the Far East," both of which were signed by Douglas MacArthur.

CHIEF COUNSEL The defense remembers that fact perfectly well. "Remember" is hardly adequate to describe our feelings. I and the defense all have serious and fundamental doubts and questions in relation to the Special Proclamation and its appendix, the Charter, signed by His Honor, General Douglas MacArthur, Supreme Commander for the Allied Powers. That is to say, the problem is one concerning the jurisdiction of the present court, and we have already submitted our motions concerning these doubts to the court in written form. We have done this because these doubts are "motions" as provided for in the Charter and because the Charter requires that "motions are to be submitted in written form."

CHIEF PROSECUTOR   Does this then mean that your motion concerning the Charter has been made in accordance with the regulations set forth therein, in accordance with the very documents about which you have serious and fundamental doubts?

CHIEF COUNSEL   Exactly. The defense has no choice but to begin from this strange position. Or rather, let us call the position shaky. It is as if we were made to doubt the existence of the very earth on which we must stand.

CHIEF PROSECUTOR   As Chief Prosecutor, I have serious and fundamental doubts in regard to any such conception as that held by the Chief Counsel. May I enter into debate concerning this question?

JUDGE A   [*finally succeeding in breaking into the debate with his gentle, or perhaps relatively ineffectual, voice*]   You will please remember that I am not the President of the tribunal and that I am seated here only to announce the decision which the members of the tribunal, with the exception of the President, made during the recess. [*The Chief Prosecutor disappears.*] Consequently—

CHIEF COUNSEL   However that may be, Your Honor, I ask you once again to listen calmly, if you will, to all the reasons for my challenge against the President. First, it is not proper, from the viewpoint of justice and fairness, that the President should conduct this trial. Secondly, it is improper for the President to conduct this trial, in accordance with the Potsdam Declaration of July 26 of last year. I shall not repeat my explanations of these points. Third, however, is the fact that the President has investigated the case of Japanese atrocities and murders

committed in New Guinea and has submitted the results
of his investigation to the government of Australia, his
homeland and a member of the Allies.

JUDGE A   The President stated previously that he did not think
that fact had any relevance to the fact that he now is
President of this tribunal.

CHIEF COUNSEL   The President had not heard a full explanation
of my challenge when he made that statement. In short,
the President submitted his report to the Australian government. The third reason for my challenge is this: It is very
inappropriate for a court which is dedicated to the two high
ideals of justice and fairness—please listen to me—it is
inappropriate that the same man who submitted a report
on atrocities committed by the Japanese in New Guinea
to this court—please wait—it is inappropriate that the
very same man should act as President of this court. Let us
set aside for the moment the fact that this court is being
carried out in the language and customs of the Anglo-
American legal system. From the point of view of the con-
tinental legal system, which Japan has followed up to now,
is it not a fact that the President of the tribunal has com-
bined in his person both judge and prosecutor? That is
impermissible under any rule of modern law. It is a contradiction. Why does the President violate this legal
principle?

CHIEF PROSECUTOR   [once again illuminated at the side of the Chief
Counsel]   If the Chief Counsel requests an explanation
for this from the President, and if the President should
open debate in response, we would find ourselves debating
a problem that is totally irrelevant to the present stage of
this trial. The Chief Counsel will please recall once again
the fact that this court is founded on two documents, the
Special Proclamation and the Charter.

JUDGE A   And consequently, I am seated here for only one
purpose, to announce the decision of the tribunal. The
members of the tribunal are of the opinion that no objection
to the person of any member of the tribunal can be sustained. For Article 2 of the Charter, which is provided for
in the Special Proclamation, clearly prescribes that the

tribunal shall consist of members appointed by General
Douglas MacArthur, Supreme Commander of the Allied
Powers and author of the Special Proclamation. That
being so, it does not rest with the tribunal to unseat anyone appointed by the Supreme Commander.

The President will now be seated.

*The Chief Counsel disappears. The highly confident face of the
President appears in place of Judge A's.*
*Behind the President, the national flags of nine Allied nations
appear—the United States, England, Holland, France, the Soviet
Union, China, Australia, New Zealand, and Canada.*

PRESIDENT   I gave serious consideration to my position before
I accepted appointment as President of this tribunal and
deemed that I was eligible, and I take added confidence
in my eligibility for this position from the support my most
reliable colleagues have shown me. We shall begin immediately with the arraignment. First, in alphabetical
order, the names of the accused—

CHIEF COUNSEL [*suddenly illuminated*]   Your Honor, I feel it is only
proper that action should be taken on the motion concerning the jurisdiction of the court which the defense submitted
in written form several days ago, before we begin with the
arraignment.

PRESIDENT   [*with ease*]   Do you intend to state the contents of
your motion concerning the jurisdiction of the court here
and now?

CHIEF COUNSEL   It is a prerequisite to any further action. If I
do not do so now, it will be too late when the pleas have
already been taken.

PRESIDENT   I intend to conduct this court with all due consideration, so that nothing will happen "too late."

CHIEF COUNSEL   Excuse me. Then as a question of priorities, I
feel that it must be stated now. The reason—

PRESIDENT   I hope the Chief Counsel will speak calmly. As you
know, this trial will continue for many more months.

CHIEF COUNSEL   Calmly? Certainly I am speaking calmly. How-

ever, I must point out that if the arraignment is completed before this motion has been submitted—

PRESIDENT   No one has said that we would not allow you to
submit that motion.

CHIEF COUNSEL   However, as Your Honor was already about to
proceed with the arraignment, I—

PRESIDENT   Please tell me the reason why you must submit your
motion now.

CHIEF COUNSEL   I am very grateful for the court's permission.
Our motion concerns the fact that this court has been
convened to try the twenty-eight defendants on three
charges of war crimes, composed of fifty-five counts. First
crimes against peace. Second, murder and conventional war
crimes. Third, crimes against humanity. We submit that
the court does not have the authority to charge the defendants with crimes against peace and crimes against
humanity. These are problems which lie outside the jurisdiction of this court. If our motion is granted, there will
be no need for half the defendants to enter any plea. Therefore, we submit that this petition is a prerequisite to any
further action.

PRESIDENT   It is open to the accused to plead conditionally.

CHIEF COUNSEL   In other words, Mr. President, does that mean
that even if we do not enter into the problem of the
court's jurisdiction immediately, the defendants may plead
under the condition that, in the future, they may contend
that their pleas lie within the scope of the motion now
being submitted to the court?

PRESIDENT   The defendant pleads once for all time. He may not
question the jurisdiction of the court in the future.[1]

---

[1]There is a discrepancy at this point between the English and Japanese original
sources. The original statement of President Webb is as follows: "He pleads once for all
time, but his plea will not prevent him from questioning the jurisdiction later if so
advised" (*International Military Tribunal for the Far East: Proceedings, 1946–1948*; p. 99).
For the same statement, the Japanese is: 認否は一回限りでありまして後日において
管轄権を疑うことが出来ません (*Kyokutō kokusai gunji saiban sokkiroku*, v. 1, p. 7).
This states just the opposite, that the jurisdiction may *not* be questioned later.

Kinoshita follows the Japanese source almost word for word: 罪状認否は一回限り
でありまして，後日において管轄権を疑うことはできません as found in *Shimpan*, p.
18 of the published text. It is possible that there was a mistake in translating the state-

CHIEF COUNSEL   What in the . . . Then I must be allowed to argue the motion now.

PRESIDENT   They may plead conditionally.

MONITOR   [*mechanically*]   Monitor's summary. The defendant pleads once for all time, but the plea may be made conditional to the motion which has been submitted.

CHIEF COUNSEL   For the record it is my understanding that the question of jurisdiction and those other special motions are reserved. It is my hope, however, that the crucial question of jurisdiction be expeditiously heard. The defense is now prepared to proceed with the arraignment.

The Chief Counsel disappears.

PRESIDENT   I now call on the accused to plead.

Following this, the President calls on each defendant to plead. The defendants, who are to be seated in the third and fourth rows of the auditorium, are seated in the following order:
Facing the stage, from the right, in the third row—Doihara, Hata, Hirota, Minami, Tōjō, Oka, Umezu, Araki, Mutō, Hoshino, Kaya, Kido, Kimura.
Facing the stage, from the right, in the fourth row—Hashimoto, Koiso, Nagano, Ōshima, Matsui, (Ōkawa's empty seat directly behind Tōjō), Hiranuma, Tōgō, Matsuoka, Shigemitsu, Satō, Shimada, Shiratori, Suzuki, Itagaki.

PRESIDENT   [*staring fixedly at each person as he calls on him*]   First, Araki Sadao. Do you plead guilty or not guilty?

ARAKI'S VOICE   [*defiantly*]   That question will be replied to by my counsel.

PRESIDENT   You are required by this court to answer in person.

---

ment into Japanese at the time of the trial. In Kinoshita's script, the Chief Counsel's next word, そんな . . . , a word indicating anger and contempt for the opponent's statement, results from the effect of the Japanese mistranslation. This attitude is not apparent in either the original English or Japanese records of the same speech by Dr. Kiyose, the actual Chief Counsel. In the original Japanese records, the mistake is made apparent within several speeches; Kinoshita uses the monitor to correct the mistake. This discrepancy is a good example of the great problem of imprecise translation that was very apparent in the early days of the actual trial.

ARAKI'S VOICE   Upon inspection of the indictment, I find that the charges which appear at the very outset concerning peace, war, and humanity would cause me to forfeit the confidence I have in my seventy years of life. Accordingly—

PRESIDENT   It is not the time to make speeches now. Do you plead guilty or not guilty?

ARAKI'S VOICE   Accordingly, I cannot submit to these charges. I plead not guilty.

CHIEF PROSECUTOR   [*suddenly illuminated*]   As representative of the prosecution, I ask the court to strike out from the record everything that was said by the accused other than the words "not guilty."

DEFENSE ATTORNEY A   [*suddenly illuminated*]   Defense objects. Counsel has not been informed of what he said. If we do not know, we cannot protect his rights. May I have a precise translation of the defendant's entire statement? [*He listens to the translation on the earphone.*] All right. [*He disappears along with the Chief Prosecutor.*]

PRESIDENT   Next, Doihara Kenji, how do you plead, guilty or not guilty?

DOIHARA'S VOICE   [*calmly*]   Not guilty.

PRESIDENT   Next, Hashimoto Kingorō, how do you plead, guilty or not guilty?

HASHIMOTO'S VOICE   [*violently*]   Not guilty.

PRESIDENT   Hata Shunroku, how do you plead, guilty or not guilty?

HATA'S VOICE   [*somewhat tense, yet still politely*]   I plead not guilty to all counts.

PRESIDENT   [*voice gradually becoming mechanical*]   Hiranuma Kiichirō, how do you plead, guilty or not guilty?

HIRANUMA'S VOICE   [*impassively*]   I plead not guilty.

PRESIDENT   Hirota Kōki, how do you plead, guilty or not guilty?

HIROTA'S VOICE   [*calmly*]   Not guilty.

PRESIDENT   Hoshino Naoki, how do you plead, guilty or not guilty?

HOSHINO'S VOICE   [*in the tone of an able bureaucrat*]   I plead not guilty.

PRESIDENT   Itagaki Seishirō, how do you plead, guilty or not guilty?

ITAGAKI'S VOICE [*in a sullen, heavy tone, reminiscent of his northeast homeland*]   Not guilty.

PRESIDENT   Kaya Okinori, how do you plead, guilty or not guilty?

KAYA'S VOICE   [*restlessly*]   I plead not guilty.

PRESIDENT   Kido Kōichi, how do you plead, guilty or not guilty?

KIDO'S VOICE [*gloomily*]   I plead not guilty.

PRESIDENT   Kimura Heitarō, how do you plead, guilty or not guilty?

KIMURA'S VOICE   [*thinly*]   I plead not guilty.

PRESIDENT   Koiso Kuniaki, how do you plead, guilty or not guilty?

KOISO'S VOICE   [*nonchalantly*]   I plead not guilty.

PRESIDENT   Matsui Iwane, how do you plead, guilty or not guilty?

MATSUI'S VOICE   [*slowly*]   I plead not guilty.

PRESIDENT   Matsuoka Yōsuke, how do you plead, guilty or not guilty?

MATSUOKA'S VOICE   [*hoarse, to the point of being incomprehensible*]   I plead not guilty on all and every count.

PRESIDENT   Minami Jirō, how do you plead, guilty or not guilty?

MINAMI'S VOICE   [*with no apparent concern*]   Not guilty.

PRESIDENT   Mutō Akira, how do you plead, guilty or not guilty?

MUTŌ'S VOICE   [*composedly*]   Not guilty.

PRESIDENT   Nagano Osami, how do you plead, guilty or not guilty?

NAGANO'S VOICE   [*abruptly*]   Not guilty.

PRESIDENT   Oka Takazumi, how do you plead, guilty or not guilty?

OKA'S VOICE   [*serenely*]   Not guilty.

PRESIDENT   Ōshima Hiroshi, how do you plead, guilty or not guilty?

ŌSHIMA'S VOICE   [*high-pitched*]   Not guilty.

PRESIDENT   Satō Kenryō, how do you plead, guilty or not guilty?

SATŌ'S VOICE   [*as if shouting*]   Not guilty.

PRESIDENT   Shigemitsu Mamoru, how do you plead, guilty or not guilty?

SHIGEMITSU'S VOICE   [*heavily and quietly*]   I plead not guilty.

PRESIDENT   Shimada Shigetarō, how do you plead, guilty or not guilty?

SHIMADA'S VOICE   [*with an old-fashioned Tokyo accent*]   Not guilty.

PRESIDENT   Shiratori Toshio, how do you plead, guilty or not guilty?

SHIRATORI'S VOICE   [*very formally*]   I plead not guilty.

PRESIDENT   Suzuki Teiichi, how do you plead, guilty or not guilty?

SUZUKI'S VOICE   [*abruptly*]   Not guilty.

PRESIDENT   Tōgō Shigenori, how do you plead, guilty or not guilty?

TŌGŌ'S VOICE   [*phlegmatically*]   I plead not guilty.

PRESIDENT   Next, Tōjō Hideki, how do you plead, guilty or not guilty?

TŌJŌ'S VOICE   [*in the familiar Tōjō style*]   On all counts I plead not guilty.

PRESIDENT   Umezu Yoshijirō, how do you plead, guilty or not guilty?

UMEZU'S VOICE   [*quietly*]   Not guilty.

PRESIDENT   The plea of Ōkawa Shūmei will be taken when he is able to appear in court.

CHIEF PROSECUTOR   [*suddenly illuminated*]   If the court please, I now offer the following documents into evidence.

We first offer, as Prosecution's Exhibit No. 1, the "Cairo Conference, December 1, 1943."

Prosecution's Exhibit No. 2, "Potsdam Declaration, July 26, 1945."

Prosecution's Exhibit No. 3, styled "Japanese Qualified Acceptance of Potsdam Declaration, August 10, 1945."

Prosecution's Exhibit No. 4, "Reply by Secretary of State Hull to Japanese Qualified Acceptance, August 11, 1945."

Prosecution's Exhibit No. 5, "Final Japanese Unqualified Acceptance, August 14, 1945."

Prosecution's Exhibit No. 6, "The Instrument of Surrender, September 2, 1945."

Prosecution's Exhibit No. 7, "Moscow Conference Agreement, December 26, 1945."

Prosecution's Exhibit No. 8, "Special Proclamation of the Supreme Commander for the Allied Powers—Establishment of an International Military Tribunal for the Far East."

Prosecution's Exhibit No. 9, "General Order No. 20,

General Headquarters, Supreme Commander for the
Allied Powers, Charter of the International Military Tribunal for the Far East."

Prosecution's Exhibit No. 10, "Rules of Procedure of the
International Military Tribunal for the Far East."

DEFENSE ATTORNEY B   [*suddenly illuminated*]   If the court please,
for the record and subsequent proceedings, the defense
objects to the introduction of these documents into evidence.
For while the prosecution contends that these documents
are simply for the record, it also appears that the prosecution, by these documents, is attempting to establish the
jurisdiction of this court to indict. It is this jurisdiction
which the Chief Counsel has previously questioned. Stated
another way, we submit that these documents are being
offered to give this court jurisdiction over crimes against
peace and crimes against humanity. It is the defense's
position that these documents do not give this court any
such jurisdiction. We therefore take exception to these documents.

PRESIDENT   The court admits these documents into evidence,
noting the exception for the record.

CHIEF COUNSEL   [*suddenly illuminated*]   The defense now desires to
raise the question concerning the time for the presentation
of evidence. Setting the arraignment on this day was ex-
ceedingly early. For instance, the defendants Itagaki and
Kimura arrived in Tokyo from the South Pacific the day
before yesterday and were able to see their attorneys on
that day for only three minutes. The defense asks for two
months for examination of evidence and preparation for
trial.   The defense also asks that the question of the court's
jurisdiction, discussed today, be considered prior to trial.

CHIEF PROSECUTOR   If the court please, the prosecution is ready
to proceed with its case-in-chief in two weeks. In this respect, we point out to the court the severe and tremendous
burden imposed upon the prosecution in preparing the documents in conformity with the charges of the indictment and preparing the translations of documents into the
Japanese language. The documents cover a period of time
encompassed in the indictment of approximately fifteen

years and an area of several thousands of miles. We propose that all motions be submitted within one week to ten days and that the court be convened again in two weeks.

DEFENSE ATTORNEY B   If the court please, two weeks is far too short a time. The thirty-four members of the prosecution have had half a year's preparation with an adequate staff of close to 100 interpreters and other workers to carry out a steady investigation. On the other hand, only yesterday afternoon were any American counsel selected by the Japanese defendants with the concurrence of their Japanese counsel. All told, there are eight of us, and none of us has been here for longer than two weeks. Moreover, until we agreed to undertake the case of these defendants on sudden orders from the War Department, we did not know, and had no way of knowing, the charges to be brought against the accused. We could not be prepared. We do not even have desks yet for those counsel who have yet to arrive. We submit respectfully, sir, that the time allotted is entirely insufficient, but we will abide by whatever the court orders and do our best under any circumstances.

PRESIDENT   The American counsel should be able to receive advice and support from the Japanese counsel. We think that a period of twenty days is sufficient, at which time the court will reconvene for commencement of trial. We also think that an early date should be fixed for disposing of the motion on jurisdiction. We will hear that motion before we reconvene. The court is adjourned until 9:30 A.M. on Monday of next week, at which time we will take up the question of jurisdiction.

The stage is darkened.
The entire stage is now fully illuminated for the first time.
The seats of the judges are set in an elevated position, rear center, and the Allied flags, now eleven, with the addition of the Philippines and India, are set out in a straight row behind them. The court staff desks (piled with documents) are set before the judges' seats on a lower level (may be omitted).
On stage left, front, is the witness stand. Three sides are surrounded by a railing. In the stand is a seat on which the witness sits.

*His left profile can be seen by the audience. The stand is equipped
with several microphones and a red light, which indicates the time
when he is to speak.*

*The large desk of the court stenographer is placed before the
witness stand (may be omitted).*

*On stage right, front, is the large desk of the chief defense at-
torneys. Between this desk and the witness stand is the large desk
of the chief prosecuting attorneys.*

*Between these two desks is a lectern with a slanted top, at which
the prosecution and defense attorneys stand in turn and speak. This
stand is equipped with several microphones and a red light. The
speakers face the judges and speak with their backs to the audience.
However, they may move freely during the actual prosecution. Offstage, left, unseen, are seats for the assistant prosecution and defense
attorneys and a glass enclosure for the translators. Above this are
seats for spectators from the Allied nations.*

*Offstage, right, unseen, are seats for reporters from the Allied
nations and from Japan. Above this are seats for Japanese spectators.*

*The first two rows of the audience are for the defense counsel; the
next two, for the defendants.*

*At stage left stands the Marshal of the court and an M.P. captain.
Several other M.P.'s are also present.*

*The major prosecution and defense attorneys move in disorder
around their respective desks. Various people meet for consultations
in low, crouching positions.*

Only the judges' seats remain empty.

MARSHAL   The defendants will enter. Order in the court!

*Everyone on the stage turns and stares at the defendants' seats
briefly, to indicate the entry of the defendants.*

MARSHAL   All members of the court will rise.

*The M.P.'s open the rear stage-left door, and the judges, dressed in
gowns, come forth in the following order: India, Holland, Canada, England, the United States, Australia, China, the Soviet
Union, France, New Zealand, and the Philippines. They are seated.*

MARSHAL   All members of the court will be seated. The International Military Tribunal for the Far East is in session and is ready to hear any matter brought before it.

CHIEF COUNSEL   The defense now addresses itself to the written motion concerning the jurisdiction of this court. The most fundamental problem is that this court does not have the authority to try the defendants on charges of crimes against peace and crimes against humanity. Needless to say, this court is founded on the Potsdam Declaration, issued on the 26th of July, 1945, which advised Japan to surrender. This Declaration was acknowledged and signed when the Instrument of Surrender was signed aboard the battleship *Missouri* in Tokyo Bay by the Allies and Japan on the 2nd of September, the same year. Consequently, the Potsdam Declaration binds not only our country but the Allies as well. I ask the court for its notice of this fact.

The Tenth Article of the Potsdam Declaration states: "Stern justice shall be meted out on all war criminals, including those who have visited cruelties upon our prisoners." In other words, this court is empowered to make charges and try what are called "war criminals" in accordance with this article, but it is not thus empowered to try those who cannot be considered war criminals. Hence, it is necessary to circumscribe rationally and strictly the limits of who are to be considered war criminals, as defined by the Potsdam Declaration. In other words—

CHIEF PROSECUTOR   Your Honor! The prosecution objects to this attitude of treating this problem in so technical a fashion. It is a mistaken attitude.

PRESIDENT   Objection overruled. The Chief Counsel has not yet finished speaking.

CHIEF COUNSEL   In other words, we must limit the interpretation of what is meant by "war criminals" to that definition which existed up to the 26th of July, 1945—in other words, up to the time when this Declaration was issued by the Allied Powers and accepted by Japan. In other words, up to that time, the meaning of "war crimes," as generally accepted by the nations of the world, was those crimes relating to the violation of the laws and rules of war—rules and customs of war. To give some concrete examples, there are four typical crimes: one, violations by belligerents; two, violations by non-belligerents; three, plunder and espionage; and four, treason. The planning and waging of war cannot be considered crimes against peace and crimes against humanity in accordance with the conception of war held by the civilized nations of the world up to July 1945.

The defense presumes that the honorable judges here, the learned judges here, are well versed in the practice of international law and are aware of such well-known books on international law as those of Oppenheim and Hall. Planning a war is not mentioned as a war crime in these books or in books of international law by prominent Japanese.

CHIEF PROSECUTOR   The prosecution objects on the same grounds as before.

PRESIDENT   The defense has not yet finished its argument. The objection is overruled.

CHIEF COUNSEL   If these are the facts—and they are—the express provisions found in the Charter of this international tribunal for crimes against peace and crimes against humanity have no meaning. That is, if the Allies do not have the authority to try these cases, neither does the Supreme Commander appointed by the Allied Powers to represent the Allied Powers have the power to consider such charges, even if—or rather, precisely because—he is the Supreme Commander. It is a maxim in law that one cannot grant authorities or powers to others which one does not possess oneself; this applies perfectly well in this case.

CHIEF PROSECUTOR   The prosecution objects. The Chief Counsel has raised this problem merely as a legal technicality and is making no attempt whatsoever to touch upon the essential problems. More precisely, we cannot believe other than that the defense is arguing technical matters alone in order to avoid touching upon essential matters. We would point out to the court that the defense has conveniently omitted some very important and relevant and, we contend, deter-

minative statements and declarations addressed to this
very subject.

CHIEF COUNSEL   Your Honor—

CHIEF PROSECUTOR   To put it another way, we would like to know
how the Chief Counsel will account for that span of years
from 1928, eighteen years ago, to last year, 1945, encompassed by the counts in the charges brought against the
accused.

CHIEF COUNSEL   In the forthcoming presentation of contrary evidence, it is our intention, Your Honor, to set forth our
view on the resolute attitude taken by Japan in the past
several decades in the face of unrelieved pressure from the
major world powers. There have been a great many mis-
understandings of this attitude, even of the very words we
have used to express ourselves. No words have been sub-
jected to greater misunderstanding by the prosecution and
by the world than the expression "Greater East Asia Co-
Prosperity Sphere" or "*Hakkō Ichiu.*"

PRESIDENT   Mr. Counsel, please confine your remarks to the
main point of your argument.

CHIEF PROSECUTOR   Your Honor, we shall of course argue this
point more fully in the course of the trial, but we would
like the court's permission to ask now for an explanation of
this phrase "*Hakkō Ichiu,*" since the Chief Counsel has, of
his own accord, presented this phrase as an example of
misunderstanding on our part.

PRESIDENT   Mr. Chief Counsel, how do you explain this phrase?

CHIEF COUNSEL   We intend to call a witness later on in order to
clarify the meaning of this phrase more fully. For the present, I would answer as follows: In the proposed plan for
Japanese-American understanding, which was the basis of
negotiation between Secretary of State Hull and Ambas-
sador Nomura in 1941, "*Hakkō Ichiu*" is translated into
English as "universal brotherhood."

CHIEF PROSECUTOR   We shall carry out a full discussion of this
when the proper time comes, but for the present, we are satisfied simply to note the phrase "universal brotherhood," a
truly willful interpretation on the part of the Chief Counsel.

CHIEF COUNSEL   Your Honor, the statement made just now by the Chief Prosecutor—

CHIEF PROSECUTOR   If the court please, we have strayed far from the original point under question, and I hope the Chief Counsel will confine his remarks to the subject we were arguing. However, there is one more thing I would like to ask. The Chief Counsel stated that no words have invited greater misunderstanding than "Greater East Asia Co-Prosperity Sphere." Now—

CHIEF COUNSEL   I believe this debate belongs to a later stage of the trial, and I would like to conclude my remarks with this observation: that the expressions "Greater East Asia Co-Prosperity Sphere" and "New East Asian Order" are unparalleled for the seeds of misunderstanding they have sown. The intrinsic content of the idea of the new order as it has been spoken of in Japan is the *kōdō* or "Imperial Way," as it is sometimes translated. I believe the spirit of the "Imperial Way" can be understood only by the Japanese. The gist of it is benevolence, righteousness, and moral courage. It respects the qualities of courtesy and honor. There is, I believe, no fundamental difference between the "Imperial Way" and democracy.

PRESIDENT   Will the Chief Counsel please return to the point under question, as the Chief Prosecutor has requested.

CHIEF COUNSEL   I understand. I ask the court to consider this statement a manifestation of my genuine feelings, which I made even though it was at the wrong stage of the trial.

Now—now then, Mr. President, my next point is something very important, and I ask your leave to speak on it at some length. As you well know, in Germany, in Nuremberg in Germany, there are war crimes trials proceeding at present, and they are based on several declarations which were made against Germany. My point is that I do not think that these same declarations can be used against Japan. The reason is that there is a very great difference between the way in which Germany surrendered and the way Japan surrendered. Germany, as you know, Mr. President, resisted to the very last; Hitler died or was killed, Göring fled from the battlefront, and Germany ultimately col-

lapsed. In the case of Germany, it was literally an unconditional surrender. In other words, as regards German war
criminals, the Allies, if I may be permitted to say so, could
just as well have punished the war criminals without trial.

The case of Japan is different. The forces of the Allied
Powers had not yet landed in Japan when the Potsdam Declaration was proclaimed. At that time, the Japanese government was still in existence, composed of His Majesty the
Emperor and a good many of the defendants present at this
trial. Moreover, the Allies issued the Declaration against
Japan under the conditions stated in Article Five: "The
following are our terms. We will abide by them." The
Potsdam Declaration proposed to Japan contained conditions; there were conditions involved. It was this that
Japan accepted, and it is this that the Allies must now observe.

It is therefore an absolute mistake to bring charges
against Japanese war criminals— that is, charges of crimes
against peace and crimes against humanity— simply because the same charges are being made at Nuremberg.
Therefore—

PRESIDENT   There is no relation between the present trials and
Nuremberg.

CHIEF COUNSEL   However, Your Honor—

CHIEF PROSECUTOR   If the court please, may the prosecution have
a word?

PRESIDENT   Mr. Chief Counsel, have you any other points to make
at the present time?

CHIEF COUNSEL   My major argument is finished, but I would like
permission to explain the point I have just made more
fully, and to make two more points as well. There are also
several additional motions to be made by the American
counsel.

PRESIDENT   If the Chief Counsel has completed his argument,
we will now hear the Chief Prosecutor. The prosecution
will confine its arguments to the points made just now by
the defense.

CHIEF PROSECUTOR   Mr. President, members of this international
military tribunal, can it be that the eleven nations rep-

resented in this court and in this prosecution, and in themselves representative of thirty-eight governments, of countries containing one-half to two-thirds of the inhabitants of
this earth, having suffered through this aggression the
loss of a vast amount of their resources and deplorable and
incalculable quantities of blood due to the crimes of murder, brigandage, and plunder, are now totally impotent to
bring to trial and punish those responsible for this world-
wide calamity; that these Allied nations, having brought
about, as they were compelled to do by sheer force, the end
of these wars of aggression, must now stand idly by and
permit the perpetrators of these offenses to remain beyond
the reach of any lawful punishment whatsoever?

PRESIDENT   Mr. Chief Prosecutor, do you think those strong expressions are fitting at this juncture?

CHIEF PROSECUTOR   Mr. President, we regard the motions of the
defense as being addressed to the body public of the world,
and we do not desire to let them go entirely unchallenged.

The motion of the accused, submitted through their representative, the Chief Counsel, attempts first to restrict
the jurisdiction of this court by the accused's construction of
the language set forth in the Potsdam Declaration. Second,
in the motion there are also other assertions or implications
that the surrender of Japan was subject to certain conditions in this respect. We are not concerned with these con-
tentions as purely technical problems of law, in the way the
Chief Counsel has argued them. But we do not intend in
this court to permit a false assertion which would limit
the jurisdiction of the court to remain unchallenged.

First of all, the surrender of the Japanese nation was
absolutely unconditional, as the documents already submitted to the court by the prosecution and those still to
be submitted clearly demonstrate. All the documents to be
submitted later, from the Potsdam Declaration to the Special Proclamation which led to the establishment of this
tribunal and the Charter of the Tribunal, show with abun-
dant clarity both that the surrender of Japan was unconditional and that the Supreme Commander for the Allied

Powers, and I quote, "is authorized to take such steps as he deems proper to effectuate the terms of surrender."

Next, we are, of course, well aware of the great difference between the capitulation of Japan and that of Germany. However, the unconditional surrender of Japan was agreed to by the duly constituted government of the Japanese nation of that time, as is clearly demonstrated by the Instrument of Surrender. If that duly constituted government had mistakenly insisted that the surrender of the authority of the Emperor and the Japanese government to the Supreme Commander for the Allied Powers was conditional, it would have been extremely simple for us to have effected the prompt and utter destruction of Japan. In fact, failure to carry forward to successful completion these proceedings on behalf of the preservation of peace could well signify the utter destruction of the world instead.

The precise legal proposition presented to this court by the defense constitutes a clear challenge to the capacity of civilized nations to take effective preventative steps to save civilization by punishing the responsible individuals who brought the scourge of aggressive warfare to a great part of the earth. The bold proposition presented by the proponents of this motion is that individuals proved to have set into motion and directed forces which brought about ruthless and unjustified war and threatened the existence of civilization are, by reason of the high official positions of responsibility which they held, immune from any punishment for such acts.

This is tantamount to a claim that a person may scatter gasoline and gunpowder throughout a building filled with human beings, stuff the closets with oil-soaked rags, pile tinder against the doors, nail the windows shut so that the occupants cannot escape, and then, having handed a torch already lighted by him to irresponsible and helpless individuals under his domination and control, order it to be applied, all with impunity.

This analogy may not be appealing to those steeped in the mustiness of legal sterilisms; but it will be understood perfectly, Mr. President, by those who bear the real suffering when war comes upon mankind and who have a right to be heard in some attempt to prevent its repetition. For the proponents of these motions claim that these leaders, directors, and officials, having obtained the power to bring this ruin and destruction about—having planned, prepared, and initiated it—can never be brought to the bar of justice. The necessary corollary follows that the helpless dupes and victims who were subject to their control and orders, as well as the millions of other innocent victims, will undergo forever the untold suffering these acts brought upon them, while these leaders remain free from punishment. And this, exactly this, is what the defense says is the law. Such a contention is as revolting as it is unsound. Is it supposed that organized society must remain supinely quiescent, with soft, folded hands of indifference, and await its own destruction in a very literal sense? That is tantamount to asserting that mankind is without lawful power to save itself.

Finally, the defense has intentionally limited its argument to the very narrow legal contention that crimes against peace and crimes against humanity were not part of the general conception of war crimes in July 1945, when the Potsdam Declaration was issued. The prosecution contends that there is not the slightest possibility of finding one person willing to recognize that proposition.

PRESIDENT I take it that the Chief Prosecutor has finished his major statement and will leave his submission of probative evidence for a later stage of the trial?

CHIEF PROSECUTOR That is correct.

CHIEF COUNSEL The defense gave notice previously that the American counsel had several additional motions to present.

PRESIDENT That, of course, means that the prosecution will present several more challenges to these motions. The court is now recessed.

The stage is dimmed and then illuminated immediately.

MARSHAL   The International Military Tribunal for the Far East is resumed.

PRESIDENT   The defense motion pertaining to the jurisdiction of this court and the additional motions which were to have followed this, are all denied for reasons to be given later.

CHIEF COUNSEL   When will the reasons for the court's decision be given?

PRESIDENT   I do not know.

CHIEF COUNSEL   If the court please, that means the defense must continue to argue its case with the most fundamental problem of the jurisdiction of this court left in reserve.

PRESIDENT   If the defense intends its present statement to be an objection, it will be overruled, as this is a decision of the court.

CHIEF COUNSEL   It is not an objection. I can only repeat what I said in the very beginning. We find ourselves in a position such that we cannot help doubting the very existence of the earth, even while we are standing on it.

CHIEF PROSECUTOR   Is that not the very work we have now begun, to insure that the foundations of the earth will not be shaken again?

PRESIDENT   The court is adjourned until a date to be fixed.

MARSHAL   The court is adjourned and will resume its session upon due notification from the President of the tribunal.

End of Act I

Act II

CHARACTERS

President of the Tribunal (Australian)
Prosecuting Attorney A (French)
Witness for the Prosecution A (French)
Defense Attorney C (American)
Defense Attorney D (Japanese)
Defense Attorney E (American)

Voice of the Language Monitor

PRESIDENT   Mr. Attorney for the Prosecution, you have called a
witness for the prosecution to the stand and have been
reading his lengthy affidavit concerning acts of atrocity
committed by Japanese forces on French military personnel
in French Indo-China. However, you have already submitted forty-some documents of evidence compiled from the
depositions of various people in French Indo-China. Don't
you agree that the present affidavit overlaps with these
documents?

PROSECUTING ATTORNEY A   Some parts overlap to a certain extent,
but the overlapping sections serve to give us a broader
picture than any single document can.

PRESIDENT   Do you intend to continue the direct examination of
your witness?

PROSECUTING ATTORNEY A   I do, in order to add a certain amount
of vividness to the documents of evidence previously submitted and also to the affidavit of this witness, which I have
just read, concerning the atrocities committed by the Japanese forces against French military personnel in French
Indo-China.

PRESIDENT   Please proceed, if you think it necessary for clarification.

PROSECUTING ATTORNEY A   Thank you. The only language which
the witness understands is his native language, French.
While French is not the official language of this court, my
right to use it in this case was established by the court last
year at the conclusion of the two-day debate in which the
prosecution proved the invasion of French Indo-China by
Japan. Are the translators ready? [*to the witness*] There are
several points in your affidavit I want to have you clarify.
First, on page one. . . . Among the various methods of
torture used by the Japanese forces, you mention indiscriminate beatings with cudgels, slivering the fingertips
under the nails with needles, burning the forehead with
cigarettes, setting people on fire with hoods doused in
gasoline, torture by water, torture by electricity, suspend-
ing a person by his thumbs. There is one method you describe whose meaning in the English translation I do not
understand: spiked wood.

WITNESS FOR THE PROSECUTION A   Spiked wood? The English translation is not accurate. Blocks of wood with sharp edges were placed on the floor, the French victim was forced to kneel on these, and a Japanese non-commissioned officer jumped on his legs. The torture was carried out in that way.

PROSECUTING ATTORNEY A   In your affidavit, you give actual examples of atrocities carried out by the Japanese forces throughout French Indo-China, from north of Hanoi to south of Saigon. Can you indicate on this map the exact place where each of these acts took place?

WITNESS FOR THE PROSECUTION A   I believe I can.

PROSECUTING ATTORNEY A   Do you believe that each of these acts of atrocity was carried out individually and separately, without relation to the other acts of atrocity?

WITNESS FOR THE PROSECUTION A   I believe that each individual act of atrocity was related to the entire activity, and that the entire activity was related to each individual act.

DEFENSE ATTORNEY C   If the court please, I object to that question as calling for a conclusion from the witness.

MONITOR'S VOICE   [*mechanically*]   The prosecutor's question was attempting to draw from the witness a conclusion which should properly be made by the court.

PRESIDENT   Objection sustained. It is for the court to decide whether each individual case was planned in relation to the others or not. Since the question was already answered, the answer given just now by the witness for the prosecution will be stricken from the court record, as the defense has requested. Does the prosecution intend to continue the direct examination?

PROSECUTING ATTORNEY A   With your permission.

PRESIDENT   You may proceed, if you think it necessary for clarification. However, I cannot allow questions like the last one. You were fishing for anything that would bite.

PROSECUTING ATTORNEY A   I want to ask the witness about the massacre at Langson. At that time, the witness—

WITNESS FOR THE PROSECUTION A   I was not yet in Langson at the time of the massacre.

PROSECUTING ATTORNEY A   Please let me finish the question first.

I want to know what happened to the bodies of those who were massacred at Langson at that time.

WITNESS FOR THE PROSECUTION A   The bodies of approximately seventy victims of the massacre were exhumed at Langson. Forty-five of these were members of the French military. Also, from the French civilian population there were five men, three women, and two children. It was evident, from the fact that the heads of some had been severed from the bodies and that ropes were still tied around the necks, that they had been hanged. All the French residents at Langson were made prisoners of war after a brief resistance against the Japanese. After that, the women and children were separated from the men and remained alive without knowing that the men had been killed. The depositions in the documents which you read were from several of those women.

PROSECUTING ATTORNEY A   Is there anything else you can remember about the massacre at Langson?

WITNESS FOR THE PROSECUTION A   I remember something I read— the deposition of a Japanese Army captain named Imuda. According to his testimony, another group of Frenchmen was taken to the river's edge outside the compound at Langson, divided into four groups, and then killed by the Japanese soldiers, at first with bayonets and swords, and after that with picks.

DEFENSE ATTORNEY D   Your Honor, a word, as a member of the defense. As a Japanese, I find it hard to believe that "Imuda" could be the name of a Japanese.

PROSECUTING ATTORNEY A   The point is not the pronunciation of the man's name, but the fact that he was an officer in the Japanese Army. The men whom the Japanese call "Torū-man" and "Dogōru" do not exist in America or France, yet we understand that you are speaking about President Truman and General De Gaulle.

PRESIDENT   Does the Japanese defense attorney intend his present remark to be an objection?

DEFENSE ATTORNEY D   No, no. I simply am not yet used to this court and only thought to ask about the name. Excuse me.

PROSECUTING ATTORNEY A   Next, I want to ask the witness about
additional facts concerning the massacre at Takhek.

DEFENSE ATTORNEY C   The defense objects. Not only are the prosecution's questions repetitive, but the witness's testimony
is based merely on hearsay and is not grounded on personal
knowledge or experience.

PRESIDENT   Hearsay evidence is admissible in this court. However,
hereafter, in seeking to supplement the witness's affidavit,
the prosecution should seek facts of greater substance
than a mere report concerning the exhuming of graves.

PROSECUTING ATTORNEY A   I have no further questions. I shall
reserve the presentation of additional facts until such time
as their greater substance can meet the expectations of the
President.

PRESIDENT   Does the defense wish to cross-examine the witness
for the prosecution?

DEFENSE ATTORNEY C   I do. However, I shall of course use
English. Are the translators ready? [*to the witness*] You
stated previously that you could indicate on the map all
of the areas which are now under question. I would like to
know where the village of Langson is.

WITNESS FOR THE PROSECUTION A   Langson is in northern Indo-
China, close to the Chinese border.

DEFENSE ATTORNEY C   And?

WITNESS FOR THE PROSECUTION A   And—that is all I know.

DEFENSE ATTORNEY C   Then please permit me to add to that. In
September 1940, the Japanese Army advanced into
French Indo-China, but only after having signed an
agreement with the French Vichy government. The first
place they passed through at that time was Langson. The
Vietnamese People's Resistance Movement also began in
this same village of Langson and quickly spread to the Red
River Delta area. The Vietnamese people took up arms and
used the following words as their slogan: "Resistance to
French and Japanese Imperialism."

PROSECUTING ATTORNEY A   The prosecution objects. The action
of the Japanese Army in 1940, which the defense has just
now called an advance into French Indo-China, was in

actuality an invasion. Also, the French Vichy government was a puppet government of the Nazis and under coercion merely gave formal recognition to the Japanese invasion. The prosecution clearly established these facts during the presentation of evidence in September of last year.

DEFENSE ATTORNEY C   The defense will formally refute these points in our presentation of rebutting evidence. The fact is that the French government at Vichy maintained normal diplomatic relations with the United States and other Allied nations at that time. In order that the court give judicial notice to this fact, the defense proposes, in our presentation of rebutting evidence—

PRESIDENT   In short, it is enough for the defense to prove its point when the time has come.

DEFENSE ATTORNEY C   Mr. Witness, I want to ask you another question. Would you please tell me once again how many bodies were exhumed from the grave of the Langson massacre?

WITNESS FOR THE PROSECUTION A   Approximately seventy.

DEFENSE ATTORNEY C   And of these seventy?

WITNESS FOR THE PROSECUTION A   Forty-five were French military. Civilians accounted for—

DEFENSE ATTORNEY C   How do you know that exactly forty-five were French military?

WITNESS FOR THE PROSECUTION A   They were wearing uniforms.

DEFENSE ATTORNEY C   I see. And civilians?

WITNESS FOR THE PROSECUTION A   There were five men, three women, and two children.

DEFENSE ATTORNEY C   Didn't you say that the three women and two children remained alive? That they remained alive and testified?

WITNESS FOR THE PROSECUTION A   They remained alive? Ah, yes, yes, my statement was not accurate.

DEFENSE ATTORNEY C   Then please state the facts accurately. Of the bodies exhumed, forty-five were French military—

WITNESS FOR THE PROSECUTION A   And five were civilian men.

DEFENSE ATTORNEY C   And?

WITNESS FOR THE PROSECUTION A   And?

DEFENSE ATTORNEY C   Please be more clear. There were forty-five bodies of French military men and five bodies of civilians. Therefore—

WITNESS FOR THE PROSECUTION A   Therefore, fifty bodies—

DEFENSE ATTORNEY C   Didn't you say before that approximately seventy bodies had been exhumed?

WITNESS FOR THE PROSECUTION A   Ah, well, the other twenty were Vietnamese. I forgot. I did not think that the bodies of Vietnamese had anything to do with this court.

DEFENSE ATTORNEY C   The Vietnamese are now fighting your homeland France. You may forget them or not; you may forget the number of their dead or not as you will. The point now in question is the fact that the bodies of twenty Vietnamese were buried together with the French in that grave.

PROSECUTING ATTORNEY A   The prosecution objects. The problem facing this court is the acts of atrocity committed by the Japanese Army. That is, in just what way did the Japanese Army massacre the French military personnel who were under the Vichy government, a government which the Japanese Army legally recognized as its rightful partner? The number of dead Vietnamese is irrelevant. The sole problem facing this court is the acts of atrocity of the Japanese Army and the evidence of these acts.

DEFENSE ATTORNEY C   I am in total agreement. The problem here at present is the acts of atrocity committed by the Japanese Army and the evidence of these acts. Therefore— please wait—therefore, will the witness please answer. Why were the twenty Vietnamese massacred along with fifty Frenchmen? Or rather, why were fifty Frenchmen massacred together with twenty Vietnamese?

WITNESS FOR THE PROSECUTION A   The fact is—the fact is that I was not there at the time of the massacre and therefore—

DEFENSE ATTORNEY C   I know that much already. I am asking you for your own personal opinion.

WITNESS FOR THE PROSECUTION A   I suppose—

DEFENSE ATTORNEY C   Yes?

WITNESS FOR THE PROSECUTION A   I suppose—that the Vietnamese were the servants of the Frenchmen.

DEFENSE ATTORNEY C   What proof do you have that the Vietnamese who were massacred were the servants of the Frenchmen who were massacred?

WITNESS FOR THE PROSECUTION A   Proof? I have no particular proof. Actually, even in Saigon, where I am living now, my servants are Vietnamese.

DEFENSE ATTORNEY C   In short, we could imagine the following case to be possible as well, couldn't we, without the slightest proof: Japanese imperialism, from the Vietnamese point of view, was quite literally the Japanese Army, and French imperialism, from the viewpoint now under consideration, was the French Regular Army under the Vichy government. These two imperialistic powers—it is immaterial that the Vietnamese are using the word imperialism with a great deal of ill-will—the Japanese government and the French Vichy government maintained relations based on international law; and in opposition to these two countries, the Vietnamese had begun a fierce resistance movement. Now, the case is that there were Frenchmen who participated in this activity along with the Vietnamese. And it seems quite possible to imagine this was the case in Langson.

WITNESS FOR THE PROSECUTION A   I have not understood the question.

DEFENSE ATTORNEY C   Why? Suppose that the Frenchmen killed at Langson were guerrillas working with the Vietnamese and were not citizens of the country which was the recognized partner of Japan. If that is so, the fact that they were killed cannot be called an act of atrocity as stated in any regulations pertaining to war. And if that is so, then we are left with a situation for which neither the Japanese Army nor its leaders, the defendants seated here, are responsible.

PROSECUTING ATTORNEY A   Your Honor, the attorney for the defense has intentionally interpreted the meaning of war crimes in a very narrow sense and is attempting to limit the problem to ordinary war crimes. He seems to have forgotten the fact that a new assertion is included in the charges brought against the defendants, an assertion that there is a war crime against humanity in a broad sense.

DEFENSE ATTORNEY C   Does this mean that the attorney for the prosecution agrees that these are not crimes, if we limit the counts to charges of ordinary war crimes?

PROSECUTING ATTORNEY A   The attorney for the defense is drawing the unwarranted conclusion—without any evidence at all—that the massacred Frenchmen were guerrillas.

DEFENSE ATTORNEY C   The word guerrilla can easily be replaced by Gaullist, if that will help. We, at least, have set forth our reasons why they could have been Gaullists, while the witness has given no reason why they might not have been so. Would the witness please answer the previous question?

PRESIDENT   It is necessary for every person in this court, and for all people in the world, to call to mind at every instant the mission of this international tribunal. We are here to make clear to the world war crimes against humanity.

DEFENSE ATTORNEY C   I have not yet received an answer to my question from the witness.

WITNESS FOR THE PROSECUTION A   Would you repeat the question?

DEFENSE ATTORNEY C   You stated that the bodies of the massacred French soldiers were dressed in uniforms. What evidence do you have that these were Vichy Regular soldiers?

WITNESS FOR THE PROSECUTION A   I do not understand the meaning of the question.

DEFENSE ATTORNEY C   Why not?

WITNESS FOR THE PROSECUTION A   Would you please repeat the question?

DEFENSE ATTORNEY C   Let me ask it this way: How can you determine who was a war criminal, unless you know which army he was fighting for?

WITNESS FOR THE PROSECUTION A   Criminals are judged by the crimes they commit.

DEFENSE ATTORNEY C   We clearly established in the previous debate that that is not the problem before us now. [*pauses*] All right, I shall repeat the question again, this way: You are a member of the War Crimes Investigation Bureau of the French Army in Indo-China. You are important enough in that organization to represent it here in the court. Do you mean to say that as a member of that bureau, you have no interest in the position your French Army took when it was fighting a few years ago in Indo-China? More precisely, does it not concern you whether the French soldiers were Gaullists or Vichyites when they were massacred by the Japanese Army?

WITNESS FOR THE PROSECUTION A I investigated only the acts of atrocity committed by the Japanese Army.

DEFENSE ATTORNEY C Mr. Witness, I cannot believe that you could possibly misunderstand the question as much as you seem to. If I may be allowed to conjecture, I would say the witness is insinuating that all the Frenchmen massacred by the Japanese Army were Vichyites.

PROSECUTING ATTORNEY A The prosecution objects. The statement of the defense is personal slander against the witness.

DEFENSE ATTORNEY C I have no further questions. My colleague will continue the cross-examination. There is, however, one final point. Mr. Witness, you stated previously that you first began investigating atrocities committed by the Japanese barely six months ago, when you took up your present position. This was already a year after the Pacific War had ended. Is this right?

WITNESS FOR THE PROSECUTION A There are many people in the Saigon War Crimes Investigation Bureau who had been investigating long before I began.

DEFENSE ATTORNEY C Mr. Witness, please answer my question. You personally began a year after the war had ended. Is that true?

WITNESS FOR THE PROSECUTION A It is.

DEFENSE ATTORNEY C Consequently, the affidavit you submitted to this court was written not from the results of direct questioning, but from knowledge you gained by reading already completed depositions.

WITNESS FOR THE PROSECUTION A I have read through all the depositions we have collected. I am the only person in the Saigon Bureau who is in a position to understand the problems involved on a broad scale and give an overall opinion about them.

DEFENSE ATTORNEY C Your Honor, I bring my cross-examination to a close with the following conclusion: Insofar as the affidavit of this witness is a description with no foundation based on direct experience or observation, it has no probative value for this court. Moreover, insofar as the affidavit contains the personal opinions and conclusions of the witness, it invades the province of the court and is therefore inadmissible.

PROSECUTING ATTORNEY A   Your Honor, I would like to have the attorney for the defense reminded that this affidavit has already been admitted by the court.

DEFENSE ATTORNEY C   However, I also remember that by the same ruling, the probative value of this affidavit was to be decided at a later time. My colleague will continue the cross-examination.

DEFENSE ATTORNEY E   Your Honor.

PRESIDENT   Mr. Attorney for the Defense.

DEFENSE ATTORNEY E   I am thankful for this opportunity to cross-examine the witness. Two or three questions will be sufficient. With no heating facilities in my rooms, the winter here has affected my throat, and I'm afraid I can't manage a long question. Please bear with me. The witness will remember that the name De Gaulle was mentioned previously by the attorney for the prosecution— [*his voice breaks*]

WITNESS FOR THE PROSECUTION A   I believe it was.

DEFENSE ATTORNEY E   That refers, of course, to General De Gaulle, hero of the French liberation and president of your country until last year.

WITNESS FOR THE PROSECUTION A   Of course. It could be no one else.

DEFENSE ATTORNEY E   Thank you for your answer. Present address?

WITNESS FOR THE PROSECUTION A   De Gaulle's present address?!

DEFENSE ATTORNEY E   No, your present address.

WITNESS FOR THE PROSECUTION A   Ah, mine. Saigon, 181 Rue Mayer—an official residence which the French Army requisitioned from the Vietnamese. Is there something more you want to know?

DEFENSE ATTORNEY E   Again, thank you for your answer. Ho

Chi Minh's resistance to the wholesale attack begun by the French last December seems to be gathering strength, doesn't it? [*his voice breaks*]

WITNESS FOR THE PROSECUTION A   Should I answer that?

DEFENSE ATTORNEY E   I didn't mean that as a question. Yesterday, your French Army finally drove Ho Chi Minh's "Capital Regiment" out of Saigon, where you presently live, after a two-month fight. Saigon was completely occupied by your French Army yesterday. I suppose you already know that.

PROSECUTING ATTORNEY A   The prosecution objects. The defense's statement has no relevance whatsoever to the witness's affidavit. Moreover, the defense—to use Your Honor's expression—is fishing for something here.

PRESIDENT   The objection is sustained on the grounds of relevance. However, I don't think the figure of speech about fishing can be applied here. How does the defense answer?

DEFENSE ATTORNEY E   I haven't got the slightest idea what kind of fish the prosecution thinks I'm going to catch here. I merely was about to congratulate the witness and his fellow countryman, the attorney for the prosecution, on the victory of the French Army in Indo-China.

PRESIDENT   The attorney for the defense will remember that the courtroom is not the place to congratulate people, just as it is not the place to go fishing.

DEFENSE ATTORNEY E   Pardon me. Let me go back to the beginning. Mr. Witness, at present, in 1947, you are living in Saigon, Indo-China. [*as if struck by a sudden thought*] Do you remember June 1940? June 1940—where were you at that time?

WITNESS FOR THE PROSECUTION A   June 1940. I couldn't forget that month. That was the month the Nazis occupied Paris.

DEFENSE ATTORNEY E   Exactly. That should be a year and month that the French will never be able to forget. Marshal Pétain, who submitted immediately to the Germans, went directly to Vichy and established the Vichy administration. In that same month, General De Gaulle broadcast the first call to the resistance movement from London and announced the beginning of the Free French movement. At that time—

PROSECUTING ATTORNEY A   The prosecution objects. This problem is of concern to France alone and has no relevance to the witness's affidavit.

PRESIDENT   Objection sustained.

DEFENSE ATTORNEY E   I was in the middle of a statement. Mr. Witness, please do not make me repeat the question. Where were you at that time?

WITNESS FOR THE PROSECUTION A   When?

DEFENSE ATTORNEY E   June 1940.

WITNESS FOR THE PROSECUTION A   Ah, when the Nazis occupied Paris. I was in Paris. I was still a student then.

DEFENSE ATTORNEY E   After that?

WITNESS FOR THE PROSECUTION A   After that, in 1941, I went to Africa, to French Equatorial Africa, as a member of the colonial government.

DEFENSE ATTORNEY E   That was as a member of the Vichy government, wasn't it? No answer? After that?

WITNESS FOR THE PROSECUTION A   After that, in 1942, I was inducted into the army.

DEFENSE ATTORNEY E   That was the Vichy Army, wasn't it? No answer? Where were you stationed?

WITNESS FOR THE PROSECUTION A   North Africa.

DEFENSE ATTORNEY E   North Africa. That means the army you entered was led by General Leclerc. Is that correct?

WITNESS FOR THE PROSECUTION A   Yes, that is correct.

DEFENSE ATTORNEY E   General Leclerc. This was the General Leclerc who later liberated Paris at the head of De Gaulle's Free French forces, in August 1944. Is that correct?

WITNESS FOR THE PROSECUTION A   Yes, it is.

DEFENSE ATTORNEY E   From what I have heard, General Leclerc was a fascinating man. Wasn't that so?

PROSECUTING ATTORNEY A   The prosecution objects. The defense's question has no relevance to the affidavit of the witness.

PRESIDENT   Objection sustained.

DEFENSE ATTORNEY E   Let me ask this question, then. The anti-Vichy forces—that is, the Gaullist Free French forces—

were headed by General Giraud, the predecessor to General Leclerc, and by the French Liberation Committee, which he had organized in French North Africa. Is it a fact that these anti-Vichy forces were overwhelmingly powerful in all the French colonies?

PROSECUTING ATTORNEY A   The prosecution objects, on the same grounds as stated in the previous objection.

PRESIDENT   Objection sustained.

DEFENSE ATTORNEY E   Let me ask a different question. [*to the witness*] Where were you transferred to after North Africa?

WITNESS FOR THE PROSECUTION A   Italy.

DEFENSE ATTORNEY E   And then?

WITNESS FOR THE PROSECUTION A   I returned to France.

DEFENSE ATTORNEY E   And then?

WITNESS FOR THE PROSECUTION A   Germany.

DEFENSE ATTORNEY E   And then?

WITNESS FOR THE PROSECUTION A   Indo-China.

DEFENSE ATTORNEY E   And then?

PROSECUTING ATTORNEY A   The prosecution objects, for the same reason as before.

DEFENSE ATTORNEY E   I withdraw the question. It was a mistake on my part, a rather humorous mistake, to have asked "and then." Indo-China. And that, in short, is why you happen to be in Saigon, Indo-China, at present, as a captain in the French Army. Now, would you please tell us about the makeup of the Free French forces in Indo-China at that time? I mean, of course, when the Vichy government was in power.

WITNESS FOR THE PROSECUTION A   My knowledge of the subject is limited. I can give you the following answer only. The anti-Vichy forces at the time when Indo-China was still under French occupation were weaker than in any other French colony.

DEFENSE ATTORNEY E   Regardless of whether they were weak or not, the fact remains that anti-Vichy forces did indeed exist in French Indo-China.

PROSECUTING ATTORNEY A   Your Honor, I object. The defense has no grounds for making these statements other than his own conjectures.

DEFENSE ATTORNEY E   Your Honor, I have very good grounds for asking these questions. We have records concerning Admiral Decoux, the Vichy Governor-General of French Indo-China, which show that he could not help but recognize the power which the secret Gaullist organization possessed in French Indo-China. Moreover, the reason he was made Governor-General was because his predecessor, General Georges Catroux, fled to London to join the Free French forces there. I am attempting to ask the witness what relation existed between him and these established facts.

PRESIDENT   Please continue with your cross-examination.

DEFENSE ATTORNEY E   Now, Mr. Witness, there is only one thing I want to ask you. During the war, did you belong to the Gaullist Free French Army or to the Vichy Army?

WITNESS FOR THE PROSECUTION A   I belonged to the French Army.

DEFENSE ATTORNEY E   For which government was that army fighting?

WITNESS FOR THE PROSECUTION A   It was fighting for France.

DEFENSE ATTORNEY E   When you say France, are you speaking of the Free France of De Gaulle, or the France of the Vichy government?

WITNESS FOR THE PROSECUTION A   I am speaking of France.

DEFENSE ATTORNEY E   When you worked for the French government before entering the army, was that the Vichy government or De Gaulle's?

WITNESS FOR THE PROSECUTION A   It was the French government.

DEFENSE ATTORNEY E   In that French government and in that French Army, were you working for De Gaulle or for the Vichy government?

WITNESS FOR THE PROSECUTION A   In the army—I was a junior officer.

DEFENSE ATTORNEY E   A junior officer of what army?

WITNESS FOR THE PROSECUTION A   The French Army.

DEFENSE ATTORNEY E   The French Army—Is there any question to which you will give me a straight answer? All right, let me ask this. In that French Army, whom did you, as military personnel, receive your pay from?

WITNESS FOR THE PROSECUTION A   The distributing officer of my
unit.

DEFENSE ATTORNEY E   Mr. Witness, I have carried out this
cross-examination with the utmost patience. Do you seriously want this court to understand from your testimony
that you were fighting for France but you didn't know
which army you were in? You insist that you were fighting
for France, but you really didn't care which army you were
in, is that it? And furthermore, you didn't know which
army you were in, is that it?

PROSECUTING ATTORNEY A   Your Honor—

WITNESS FOR THE PROSECUTION A   I did not come all this way for
anything so senseless—to be drawn into this silly game!

DEFENSE ATTORNEY E   Then what did you come for? I ask you
these questions because that is the only conclusion I can
draw.

PROSECUTING ATTORNEY A   I object. The defense—

DEFENSE ATTORNEY E   Ordinary society may allow a Frenchman
who was a member of the Vichy Army during the war to
hide that fact now, but he will not be allowed to do so in
this court. I—

PROSECUTING ATTORNEY A   I was still speaking.

WITNESS FOR THE PROSECUTION A   I—I believe there is some misunderstanding here. I was in the army under the Vichy
government as—as a matter of form. I was with the Vichy
as a matter of form. I was—I was waiting there—to put it
precisely—waiting for the next opening. Or rather, I was
waiting to see how I would change according to the conditions.

DEFENSE ATTORNEY E   I have understood quite well. You were
Vichy. That's quite enough.

PROSECUTING ATTORNEY A   The attorney for the defense is forcing
the witness to make highly personal statements. There
is no reason for the court to allow him to force confessions
of a personal nature from the witness. These have no relevance to the witness's affidavit. Furthermore, I object to
the defense's references to Vichy France and Free France.
That problem is of no concern to anyone except the French.

PRESIDENT   The first part of the objection is sustained. A personal investigation of the witness is irrelevant.

DEFENSE ATTORNEY E   However, Your Honor, it was none other than the witness himself who forced me into making him say what he did.

PRESIDENT   The second half of the objection is overruled. The fact that two governments actually did exist in France during the war obviously is relevant to the affidavit.

DEFENSE ATTORNEY E   I would now like to present the defense's conclusions.

DEFENSE ATTORNEY D   Before that, Your Honor, I would like to ask a question. [to the witness] Mr. Witness, you have testified as follows in the latter part of your affidavit: "Colonel Tsuneyoshi further stated that General Dobashi, Commander-in-Chief of the Japanese troops in Indo-China, declared to Tsuneyoshi in these very words: 'Act as if I knew nothing about it,' when Tsuneyoshi reported the massacre of the prisoners at Langson to him." Does this mean that when General Dobashi heard about the massacre at Langson he was afraid that other people might know that he himself was connected in some way with it?

WITNESS FOR THE PROSECUTION A   I am only repeating what Colonel Tsuneyoshi said in his deposition. I have added no comment to it.

DEFENSE ATTORNEY D   Then was it your interpretation that General Dobashi was afraid to report this massacre to the central authorities in Tokyo—was afraid that this massacre would be reported to the central army authorities in Tokyo?

WITNESS FOR THE PROSECUTION A   All I did was read the deposition of Colonel Tsuneyoshi.

DEFENSE ATTORNEY D   If the court please, I would like to ask one more question. In Japanese, there is a saying, "*Gankō shihai ni tessuru.*" It means that a man of great perception and insight can understand all the unstated implications of anything he reads. Now, when you read that deposition, didn't you, with your great perception, read it to mean that General Dobashi would have stopped that report short when it reached him and would not have sent it on to Tokyo?

WITNESS FOR THE PROSECUTION A   All I did was read the deposition of Colonel Tsuneyoshi.

DEFENSE ATTORNEY D   Forgive me. Most likely, I believe, the translator was not able to render to you the precise meaning of what I said.

DEFENSE ATTORNEY E   In conclusion, first, not only is there a total absence of proof that the Frenchmen massacred by the Japanese were Vichy Regular Army, but also there is good reason to believe that they may have been Gaullist guerrillas. Secondly, whether or not the witness insists that they were Vichy regulars, the fact remains that the witness himself was Vichy and therefore his testimony is of no probative value. Consequently, the Frenchmen massacred here—this has no relation to how many Vietnamese may have been killed—cannot claim rights as prisoners of war under international law. If the court please, at this time I move to strike and disregard all the evidence presented of atrocities allegedly committed by the Japanese military in Indo-China from the court record.

PRESIDENT   We will, at the proper time, pass judgment on the evidence we have heard.

End of Act II

Act III

CHARACTERS

President of the Tribunal (Australian)
Prosecuting Attorney B (English)
Prosecuting Attorney C (Russian)
Defense Attorney F (American)
Defense Attorney G (American)
Defense Attorney H (Japanese)
Clerk of the Court (American)
Marshal of the Court (American)

PRESIDENT   Mr. Attorney for the Defense, how would you answer if you were asked to summarize the argument you have presented so far?

DEFENSE ATTORNEY F   I would submit that a pact may fall into desuetude as the result of repeated violations.

MONITOR [*mechanically*]   If an international treaty has frequently been violated by signatory nations, and furthermore, if the violators have not been blamed by any of the other signatory nations, then that international treaty falls into desuetude as a result of the repeated violations.

PRESIDENT   Does the attorney for the prosecution from the United Kingdom of Great Britain and Northern Ireland have an objection?

PROSECUTING ATTORNEY B   Not an objection, but a rebuttal.

PRESIDENT   Would you please wait a little longer with your rebuttal? I interrupted the defense with my question while he was still in the midst of his argument.

DEFENSE ATTORNEY F   Probably the most obvious example of what I mean is the Kellogg-Briand Pact, commonly called the Pact of Paris, which was officially concluded in 1928 as a treaty to renounce war. I shall refer to this simply as the Kellogg Pact. In Appendix B of the prosecution's lengthy indictment is found a list of international treaties, of which the Kellogg Pact is one of the most important, and certainly the most important to be violated by Japan. However, the fact is that this important anti-war treaty has often been violated by a great number of nations.

PROSECUTING ATTORNEY B   The first nation to do so was Japan, by its act of aggression in Manchuria.

DEFENSE ATTORNEY F   We are not concerned here with which nation violated this treaty in what order. What does concern us is the fact that of all the nations which have violated this treaty, Japan alone is being attacked for that reason— attacked by this very court. Furthermore—

PROSECUTING ATTORNEY B   Your Honor—

DEFENSE ATTORNEY F   I was still speaking. Furthermore, Your Honor, it is our intention to show that there should be no reason for Japan to be attacked in this way. Which nations have sent prosecuting attorneys to this court? Five great nations from among those which won the war. Yet these very same five nations have violated the Kellogg Pact and have not been attacked for their violations. If the defense can prove this satisfactorily, there is no reason then why Japan, the sixth great signatory nation, should be attacked.

PRESIDENT   The attorney for the defense knows, of course, that the Kellogg Pact lacked any means of restraining signatory nations that might begin wars of aggression. I assume you are speaking with this knowledge in mind.

DEFENSE ATTORNEY F   There is something involved here that is more important than the presence or absence of means of restraint. International law and international treaties are not given their substance merely by the words of their texts. They are shaped by the conduct of their signatory member nations, particularly by the great nations. This is the fundamental truth: that the conduct of nations at large, and of the great nations in particular, is the criterion of international law, of international morality.

PROSECUTING ATTORNEY B   The prosecution objects.

DEFENSE ATTORNEY F   Please allow me to add one more fact. My own country, the United States of America, is one of those great nations which have violated the Kellogg Pact.

PRESIDENT   The attorney for the prosecution from the United Kingdom of Great Britain and Northern Ireland.

MONITOR [*mechanically*]   The attorney for the prosecution from the United Kingdom of Great Britain and Northern Ireland will from now on be called the English attorney for the prosecution.

PROSECUTING ATTORNEY B   The prosecution objects on the following grounds. When one nation is being prosecuted on the basis of an international treaty which was concluded by many nations, the important fact—or rather, the sole fact of our concern—is that this one nation alone is being prosecuted. We submit that it is entirely irrelevant whether or not there were any breaches by other countries of those treaties which were violated by the defendants. It is also irrelevant whether or not any other country which may have violated these treaties is a party to these proceedings.

DEFENSE ATTORNEY F   I take this to mean that the learned attorney for the prosecution has challenged me to a debate on the general and fundamental principles of international law and treaties. I am fully prepared to answer him with the following argument, which I quote from authoritative interpretation of international law: As the frequency of treaty violations by signatory nations increases, the legal significance of that treaty is diminished and the crime of the violator is lightened.

PRESIDENT Will the attorney for the defense please wait. The objection of the prosecution is sustained for the following reason. The present court's objective, as provided for in the Charter of the Tribunal, is to judge only those war criminals who have been designated "major" war criminals in that charter. This court has been established as the place for the Allied nations to prosecute Japan for its war crimes.

DEFENSE ATTORNEY F A figure of speech which the President used on an earlier occasion could easily be applied to the statements made just now by Your Honor, the President, and the attorney for the prosecution. Namely, even if a person who prosecutes a thief is a thief himself, that fact in no way helps to absolve the thief under prosecution. What you say may be very true, but I find it strange that from the outset one thief should judge another.

PRESIDENT Quite often we explain facts through the use of a figure of speech, but I do not find it desirable to force facts to conform to a figure of speech which has already been made.

DEFENSE ATTORNEY F Therefore, I have said from the beginning, let us deal with the facts, and with this fact in particular: that a great number of nations violated the Kellogg Pact. I have already submitted many documents pertinent to this fact, and I ask the court to accept them as evidence.

PROSECUTING ATTORNEY B The prosecution must by all means repeat its objection. By sustaining the objection we raised previously, the President of the tribunal has made it clear that an investigation of those violations has no bearing on the indictment brought against the defendants.

DEFENSE ATTORNEY F Your Honor—

PRESIDENT The objection of the prosecution is sustained. I would

have the defense recall once again that we are attempting
to judge only one war of aggression here. We are doing
nothing more than to inquire into one and only one war.

DEFENSE ATTORNEY F   Your Honor, I—

PROSECUTING ATTORNEY B   Our jurisdiction is limited to judging
the acts of the one country which has been brought before
us. To broaden our inquiry to each act of other countries
that may have violated the treaties and to investigate
these acts is completely beyond the jurisdiction of this court.
Moreover—
                                                                .

DEFENSE ATTORNEY F   The defense is in complete agreement with
the opinion of the prosecution. The defense has no interest
whatsoever in investigating—the prosecution has used that
word twice now—the acts of aggression carried out by the
Union of Soviet Socialist Republics in the State of Manchuria, for example.

PROSECUTING ATTORNEY B   I was not finished.

DEFENSE ATTORNEY F   If the present court concludes that such acts
as these, carried out by the great nations, are not criminal
acts of aggression, the defense cannot but take the greatest
interest in this.

PROSECUTING ATTORNEY B   As I was saying, not only are these acts
completely outside the jurisdiction of the present court,
but also, if we should widen the investigation in the way the
defense suggests, there would be no end to it, and finally
we would only be forced to bring unforeseen problems
under examination.

DEFENSE ATTORNEY F   The defense wishes to know what is meant
by "unforeseen problems."

PRESIDENT   The objection of the prosecution is sustained.

DEFENSE ATTORNEY F   Your Honor, please let me ask my question.
What did the prosecution mean by "unforeseen problems"?

PROSECUTING ATTORNEY B   I do not believe it necessary to bring
such problems into question now.

DEFENSE ATTORNEY F   I do. I must know what you meant in order
to answer your argument clearly.

PROSECUTING ATTORNEY B   Then I shall say what I meant: the
dropping of the atomic bomb. We would only be forced to

bring under examination the use of the atomic bomb by the United States of America, your homeland.

DEFENSE ATTORNEY F   Therefore . . . therefore, as I said, neither I nor the defense has any interest in "investigation."

PRESIDENT [to Defense Attorney G, who has walked up to the speaker's lectern and is standing there hesitantly]   Does the attorney for the defense from America have an objection?

DEFENSE ATTORNEY G   No, I have simply walked up to the lectern.

PRESIDENT   I do not think this courtroom is the appropriate place for taking a walk.

DEFENSE ATTORNEY G   Nor is this the appropriate time for a walk. I will go back.

PROSECUTING ATTORNEY C   Until our American colleague has found the appropriate time and place for his walk, the attorney for the prosecution from the Union of Soviet Socialist Republics would like the floor.

PRESIDENT   The attorney for the prosecution from the Union of Soviet Socialist Republics.

MONITOR [mechanically]   The attorney for the prosecution from the Union of Soviet Socialist Republics will be called the Soviet attorney for the prosecution.

PROSECUTING ATTORNEY C   Since I speak only Russian, you will, I hope, understand that my response to the debate is necessarily a little slow. I would like to ask the American attorney for the defense about something he said previously. If the present court concludes that the acts of state of the several great powers after the 1928 Kellogg-Briand Peace Pact was concluded are not criminal acts of aggression—if they are not, what does the American attorney for the defense then say?

PRESIDENT   Has the Soviet attorney for the prosecution taken the floor in order to question the attorney for the defense?

PROSECUTING ATTORNEY C   No, in order to make an objection. I am asking this question as a preliminary to my objection.

PRESIDENT   Will the American attorney for the defense please answer the Soviet attorney for the prosecution's question?

DEFENSE ATTORNEY F   If the present court concludes that the acts of state of the several great powers which are signatories of the Kellogg Pact are not criminal acts of aggression, then I meant to say the defense cannot but take the greatest interest in this.

PROSECUTING ATTORNEY C   I believe what you mean by your statement is that you cannot but have the greatest doubts about this. For if the present court were to conclude that all these acts *were* criminal acts of aggression and, furthermore, that no restraints could be imposed on the signatory nations, the criminal acts of aggression of Japan also would be justified and wiped away by the same logic.

DEFENSE ATTORNEY F   We are honored by the Soviet attorney for the prosecution's generous interpretation, which goes well beyond the intention of the defense.

PROSECUTING ATTORNEY C   However—or rather, for that reason—the argument of the American attorney for the defense is nothing other than sophistry, aimed at an unwarranted justification of the Japanese position. It seems the defense attorney previously made reference to the relations between the Union of Soviet Socialist Republics and the State of Manchuria. It was made clear when the prosecution tendered its evidence that not a single criminal act of aggression ever occurred between these two countries.

DEFENSE ATTORNEY F   The acts in which I said the defense would take great interest were those not only of the Union of Soviet Socialist Republics but of all the other signatory nations as well.

PRESIDENT   Does the Soviet attorney for the prosecution mean his statement to be a motion for objection?

PROSECUTING ATTORNEY C   I do, an objection to the sophistry of the American attorney for the defense.

PRESIDENT   I find this very strange. Your objection contradicts the objection raised previously by your colleague, the English attorney for the prosecution. He objected outright to the defense's argument, on the grounds that it was irrelevant to the indictment brought against the defendants. You, however, would recognize that argument as relevant and then object to one particular case which the defense has mentioned.

PROSECUTING ATTORNEY B   My colleague, the Soviet attorney, will take the opportunity to reopen this question during his cross-examination of the defense.

PRESIDENT Please return to the point in question.

DEFENSE ATTORNEY F The point now in question is whether or not the court recognizes the instances for which I have tendered documentary evidence as criminal acts of aggression. I would like to begin the procedure by reading the evidence for each case.

PROSECUTING ATTORNEY B Your Honor, the prosecution objects.

DEFENSE ATTORNEY F Mind you, I am not asking the court to "investigate" each and every case. I am only requesting it to take judicial notice.

PROSECUTING ATTORNEY B If, in so doing, the court judges these cases to be criminal acts of aggression, then—as the Soviet attorney for the prosecution pointed out—the defense will most likely argue that the criminal acts of aggression committed by Japan are justified by this and that Japan should be exonerated. If, on the other hand, the court judges these cases not to be criminal acts of aggression, then the defense will argue that Japan is innocent for the same reason. Really, that is the most transparent sophistry.

DEFENSE ATTORNEY F We are honored by the deep insight of the English and Soviet attorneys. However, the truth is that their own arguments are highly sophistical. Their contention can in no way hinder me from following this legal procedure in accordance with the court regulations. Your Honor, I have no other recourse than to submit these documents according to the proper procedures. I must ask you to judge each case separately for its relevance to the present hearing.

PRESIDENT We cannot shut out a single relevant and material fact, no matter how disagreeable, unless it is cumulative or petty. The court will be recessed briefly, during which time I shall confer with my colleagues on the question of whether you may tender these documents as evidence.

DEFENSE ATTORNEY G Your Honor.

PRESIDENT The court is about to be recessed. I think you would do best to enjoy a walk in the lobby for the defense.

DEFENSE ATTORNEY G   Your Honor, the course of the debate has made clear to me the purpose of my walk, and so I have no more need to take it. If Your Honor please, I would like to take an exception to the ruling of the court, however the court may rule on these documents after the recess.

PRESIDENT   Your exception should be made after the ruling.

DEFENSE ATTORNEY G   I am making the exception now, because there is a particular document that I want to submit.

PRESIDENT   We shall examine the question at the proper time.

DEFENSE ATTORNEY G   Your Honor will please remember that I will be submitting one document later based on that exception.

PRESIDENT   The court is recessed.

The stage is darkened and then lit again.

MARSHAL OF THE COURT   The International Military Tribunal for the Far East is now resumed.

PRESIDENT   The decision is a decision of the majority. The court finds all the documents submitted by the defense to be immaterial and irrelevant. However, as a matter of procedure, the court has decided that it is necessary to listen to a reading of those documents, however disagreeable that procedure may be.

DEFENSE ATTORNEY F   I am of course very thankful for the court's ruling, but I must point out that I do not consider this procedure to be merely a disagreeable formality. If Your Honor please, I still intend to offer these documents and let the court's ruling apply to each one of them separately, as has been done in similar instances in the past. I believe this is necessary in order to protect future rights.

PRESIDENT   Tender them and we shall reject them, in accordance with the decision of the majority.

DEFENSE ATTORNEY F   [*mechanically, for the duration of the submission*] The first is Defense Document No. 475, the Journal of the League of Nations. I request that it be marked for identification.

CLERK OF THE COURT   [*mechanically, for all his lines in the act*]   Defense Document No. 475 will be given exhibit No. 2323 for identification only.

DEFENSE ATTORNEY F   This document concerns the action of the Council of the League.

PRESIDENT [*mechanically, and continues so for the duration of the submission*]   The court rejects this.

DEFENSE ATTORNEY F   Next is Defense Document No. 478. I request that it be marked for identification.

CLERK OF THE COURT   Defense Document No. 478 will be given exhibit No. 2324 for identification only.

DEFENSE ATTORNEY F   I now offer in evidence excerpts therefrom, which consist of parts of the speech of Winston Churchill in the House of Commons on the 9th of September, 1941, dealing with the subject of the occupation of Iran.

PRESIDENT   The court rejects this.

DEFENSE ATTORNEY F   Next is Defense Document No. 559. I request that it be marked for identification.

CLERK OF THE COURT   Defense Document No. 559 will be given exhibit No. 2325 for identification only.

DEFENSE ATTORNEY F   The above document was published by the United States Department of War Printing Office. It concerns the outbreak of World War II.

PRESIDENT   The court rejects this.

DEFENSE ATTORNEY F   Next is Defense Document No. 563. I request that it be marked for identification.

CLERK OF THE COURT   Defense Document No. 563 will be given exhibit No. 2326 for identification only.

DEFENSE ATTORNEY F   This document consists of the Treaty of Non-Aggression between the U.S.S.R. and Estonia. It was published by the Foreign Ministry of Japan.

PRESIDENT   The court rejects this.

DEFENSE ATTORNEY F   Next is Defense Document No. 561. I request that it be marked for identification.

CLERK OF THE COURT   Defense Document No. 561 will be given exhibit No. 2327 for identification only.

DEFENSE ATTORNEY F   This is an excerpt concerning Romania from the above exhibit No. 2325.

PRESIDENT   The court rejects this.

DEFENSE ATTORNEY F   Next is Defense Document No. 516. I request that it be marked for identification.

CLERK OF THE COURT   Defense Document No. 516 will be given
exhibit No. 2328 for identification only.

DEFENSE ATTORNEY F   I now offer in evidence of the occupation
of Timor the *New York Times* for the 20th of December,
1941, Defense Document No. 516. This issue of the
New York Times contains a speech of protest by Premier and
Foreign Minister Antonio de Oliveira Salazar made
against the occupation of Portuguese Timor by Holland
and Australia, the President's homeland.

PRESIDENT   The court rejects—

PROSECUTING ATTORNEY B   If Your Honor please, for the most
part this document has no relevance whatsoever to this
trial, as is the case with all the other documents tendered
so far. However, one portion of this document has great
relevance, for it bears evidence of a conspiracy on the part
of the defendants.

DEFENSE ATTORNEY G   Your Honor, that particular portion of this
document has no relevance to this trial.

PRESIDENT   The defense, which has so far argued that the documents are relevant, now argues that this document is
irrelevant.

DEFENSE ATTORNEY G   That is, of course, only for that one portion.

PRESIDENT   And the prosecution, which has so far argued that the
documents are irrelevant, now argues that this one is
relevant.

PROSECUTING ATTORNEY B   That is, of course, only for that one
portion.

PRESIDENT   Then will the prosecution first demonstrate the
relevancy of that one portion, and following that, will the
defense please demonstrate its irrelevancy? The judges will
remain neutral.

PROSECUTING ATTORNEY B   In this article, the Berne correspondent
for the *New York Times* reports the following summery of a
speech made on the 19th of December by Premier Salazar
in the Portuguese National Assembly: "Wednesday morning, two days ago, two armed contingents that appear to
have been of Australian and Dutch nationalities debarked
forcibly at Dili, invoking as their reason the defense of Java,
Sumatra, Borneo, the Celebes, and other Dutch colonies to

the north and Australia to the south from imminent Japanese aggression." The fact is that the Japanese did land on Timor, a mere two months later. We have here clear proof of a conspiracy on the part of the defendants, a—

DEFENSE ATTORNEY G   If Your Honor please, the attorney for the prosecution has deliberately omitted the last part of the speech by Premier Salazar as reported in this article. According to the prosecution's presentation, Premier Salazar gave credence to the explanation the Dutch and Australians offered for this forced landing—that it was a measure taken to defend their homeland and colonies. This, however, is not the case at all. The article continues as follows: "Dr. Salazar acknowledged that the island, which lies between Australia and the Dutch Indies, was of 'greatest importance to the defense of Australia,' but asserted that a Japanese attack there could not be regarded as 'probable.'" Premier Salazar's speech clearly denies any conspiracy on the part of the defendants.

PROSECUTING ATTORNEY B   I did indeed deliberately omit the last part of Premier Salazar's speech, as the attorney for the defense has phrased it. I did so out of a sense of respect for Premier Salazar. His last words indicate nothing more than that his judgment at that time, if I may be so bold as to say so, was badly mistaken.

DEFENSE ATTORNEY G   Your Honor, when Premier Salazar here says Wednesday morning, two days ago, he means the 17th of December, 1941, a mere nine days after Japan had opened hostilities against the United States. How can a mere nine days prove a conspiracy on the part of the defendants? We claim that, on the contrary, this document indicates nothing more than one and only one fact: that already, at that early date, Australia, the President's homeland, and the Netherlands had occupied Portuguese Timor. It indicates nothing more than that one fact.

PROSECUTING ATTORNEY B   If I may, I repeat that the Japanese occupied Timor a mere two months later, immediately after taking Singapore.

PRESIDENT   I remind the defense that it is immaterial to this affair whether or not my homeland is Australia. The defense seems to take great pains to point out the homeland of each and every one of us. I find this unnecessary—

DEFENSE ATTORNEY G   Your Honor, the defense contends that once war was underway, the Japanese attacked the enemy wherever they found them, and that occupation of enemy territory alone in no way constitutes evidence of a conspiracy on the part of the Japanese.

PROSECUTING ATTORNEY B   Your Honor, I am speaking of a relation between facts, not of single facts alone. The Australians and the Dutch first stationed soldiers on Timor, and then the Japanese occupied it soon afterward. I am not speaking merely of the fact that the Japanese occupied Timor. If that were all, it would have no more relevance to a charge of conspiracy than the fact that the Americans and the English stationed soldiers on Greenland and Iceland.

DEFENSE ATTORNEY G   If the court please, once again I—

PRESIDENT   I have just now received memoranda from my colleagues concerning this problem. The crime of conspiracy is related to all fifty-five counts and is being prosecuted in all three divisions of those counts, namely, crimes against peace, murder and conventional war crimes, and crimes against humanity. The crime of conspiracy is being prosecuted throughout the entire period of time from 1928 and the Manchurian problem to 1945 and the signing of the statement of surrender. Following the majority decision of my colleagues, we have decided to admit that document on the usual terms.

CLERK OF THE COURT   The excerpt from Defense Document No. 516, bearing the same number, will receive exhibit No. 2328A.

DEFENSE ATTORNEY F   I am highly displeased that only that part of the whole document which is detrimental to the defense should be admitted as evidence. Next is Defense Document No. 517. I request that it be marked for identification.

CLERK OF THE COURT   Defense Document No. 517 will be given exhibit No. 2329 for identification only.

DEFENSE ATTORNEY F   This article from the *New York Times* concerns America's role as protector of Iceland.

PRESIDENT   The court rejects this.

DEFENSE ATTORNEY F   Next is Defense Document No. 518. I request that it be marked for identification.

CLERK OF THE COURT   Defense Document No. 518 will be given exhibit No. 2330 for identification only.

DEFENSE ATTORNEY F   I offer in evidence the excerpt therefrom which consists of the message of President Roosevelt to Congress in relation to Iceland.

PRESIDENT   The court rejects this.

DEFENSE ATTORNEY F   Next is Defense Document No. 562. I request that it be marked for identification.

CLERK OF THE COURT   Defense Document No. 562 will be given exhibit No. 2331 for identification only.

DEFENSE ATTORNEY F   This consists of excerpts from the book *Events Leading up to World War II* which relate to the Greenland matter.

PRESIDENT   The court rejects this. Does this conclude your submission?

DEFENSE ATTORNEY F   It does. My colleague will now take the floor.

DEFENSE ATTORNEY G   My colleague for the defense argued that international law is defined not by the texts of treaties but by the acts of state of the signatory nations. To support his argument he then tendered a number of documents concerning the acts of state of several nations bound by treaties, and finally buried these documents in a tedious ceremony. I would now like to present one more document as a requiem to that ceremony. My right to do so is grounded on the motion of exception which I made before the recess. I tender Defense Document No. 553, an article from the *Nippon Times* dated the 20th of February, 1947, and request that it be marked for identification.

CLERK OF THE COURT   Defense Document No. 553 will be given exhibit No. 2332 for identification only.

PRESIDENT   What does this concern?

DEFENSE ATTORNEY G   And I offer in evidence the excerpt therefrom bearing the same document number.

PRESIDENT   What is this article concerned with?

DEFENSE ATTORNEY G   The article is entitled "America's Decision to Drop the Bomb."

PROSECUTING ATTORNEY B   Your Honor—

DEFENSE ATTORNEY G   The article is an account by former Secretary of War Stimson of the reasons why the United States used the A-bomb in the last stages of the Pacific War.

PROSECUTING ATTORNEY B   Your Honor—

DEFENSE ATTORNEY G   Furthermore, Mr. Stimson is the man ultimately responsible for the dropping of the bomb.

PROSECUTING ATTORNEY B   Your Honor—

DEFENSE ATTORNEY G   The English attorney for the prosecution will remember that he previously mentioned the bomb. The document I am now offering is not merely relevant to that problem. It places that problem directly before this court, and the court will no longer be able to avoid passing judgment on it.

PROSECUTING ATTORNEY B   Your Honor, the prosecution has not yet had the opportunity to see this document, which the defense submitted so precipitously. However—

DEFENSE ATTORNEY G   When the defense raised the same objection once before, the President made the following ruling based on the court regulations: This court is not empowered to request or coerce either party to distribute to the opposite party *prior to submission* any document already admitted by the court.

PRESIDENT   It may be true that there have been several instances where an opening statement was submitted by reading prior to distribution, but that was simply because we did not have sufficient paper to print it in time.

PROSECUTING ATTORNEY B   Your Honor, we have not yet had the opportunity to see this document, but we feel certain that it falls within the scope of the objection I raised to the entire series of documents previously submitted.

PRESIDENT   However, this document has been submitted just now for the first time.

PROSECUTING ATTORNEY B   Then, once again, I must raise the same objection for the same reasons. The choice of weapons on the Allied side in the war has no bearing upon any issue before this court. It certainly can have no bearing on the charges which have been laid before this court, the charges of conspiracy or planning of war, and of initiating or waging war.

DEFENSE ATTORNEY G   I will not accept the logic which you used
before in your argument with my colleague. I will not try
to "investigate" each and every case of each and every
country as a vain and hopeless gesture. I am speaking of
one single case, the dropping of the atomic bomb. Previously I was warned by the President that I was overusing the
word "homeland," but I firmly believe there is great meaning in using that word in this case. The defendants are
being asked to account for their alleged violations of the
Hague Convention. Yet in that same Hague Convention,
in the fourth part, the Laws and Customs of War on
Land, there is a law prohibiting the use of certain types of
weapons, namely, weapons like the atomic bomb; and by
dropping the bomb, the United States of America violated
that treaty and clearly committed a war crime. The defense
is thus forced to ask the United States of America, which is
the homeland of the members of the defense, how it accounts for its act of dropping the bomb. Of course, as a
separate question, I think the court would be entitled to
draw the conclusion from this document that the Hague
Convention of 1907 is obsolete.

PRESIDENT   I warn the attorney for the defense that I do not think
it is proper to call the Hague Convention obsolete, even
provisionally. The Hague Convention has been cited in the
indictment as one of the major international treaties which
give this court its legal foundation.

DEFENSE ATTORNEY G   As I was saying, if we concede that officials
of Japan were violating the Fourth Hague Convention by
conspiring to wage war, as they have been charged, we will
find ourselves in a dilemma. For we find that high officials
of the United States, my homeland, were already planning
to use this weapon in 1941, the year Japan carried out its
attack on Pearl Harbor. I have submitted this document as
proof of that fact. What does the court think of this? I and
the entire defense staff find we are brought face to face with
an impossible dilemma, wherein two countries have violated a treaty, and one country is prosecuting the other for
its violation.

PROSECUTING ATTORNEY B   Prosecution objects. I believe that the defense has intentionally confused the issue. The question of whether dropping the bomb is a war crime or not has absolutely no relevance to this trial.

DEFENSE ATTORNEY G   If the Hague Convention is obsolete, that is so. But if it is not obsolete, as the President has said, then dropping the bomb is a war crime, against which Japan has the recognized right to retaliate. And if that is so, the question of the bomb has great relevance to this trial.

PROSECUTING ATTORNEY B   Even if this right to retaliate is applicable, even granting that argument, that still does not justify Japanese war crimes committed before the bomb was dropped.

DEFENSE ATTORNEY G   No one has said anything about using the bomb to justify Japan's actions before it was dropped. The defense will demonstrate the innocence of the defendants prior to the dropping of the bomb by other evidence.

PRESIDENT   Suppose that we were to recognize the defense's argument. What actions of Japan after the bomb was dropped would the defense attempt to exonerate by the right of retaliation?

DEFENSE ATTORNEY G   Everything we would exonerate is included in the prosecution's indictment.

PROSECUTING ATTORNEY B   If the court please, I remind the defense that the time covered in the indictment is approximately seventeen continuous years. This period of time cannot be divided before and after the dropping of the bomb to suit the convenience of the defense.

DEFENSE ATTORNEY G   Your Honor, the present statement of the prosecution has no relevance whatsoever to my submitting that the dropping of the atomic bomb is relevant to this trial.

PRESIDENT   I do not believe it is the proper time for the court to make a ruling on this question. At any rate, the war ended a mere week after the bomb was dropped, didn't it?

DEFENSE ATTORNEY G   The fact that the two bombs dropped on Japan caused an immediate termination of the war one week later cannot be denied. However, our investigation shows that the decision to drop the bombs was made by

July the 22nd, 1945, at the latest. If there is any doubt
about this, we are prepared to tender the results of our
investigation as evidence any time. The 22nd of July makes
it three weeks to the end, not one.

PRESIDENT   That still leaves you with a period of only three weeks.

DEFENSE ATTORNEY G   However, those three weeks might be
enough to prove the innocence of one of the defendants.
My recollection is that the evidence covering those three
weeks was rather voluminous. In the case of Manila, for
example—

PROSECUTING ATTORNEY C   Your Honor—

PRESIDENT   Will the Soviet attorney for the prosecution please
wait for a moment? Mr. Attorney for the Defense, you
would establish the legitimacy of Japan's position by means
of a very questionable hypothesis—namely, that your
homeland, the United States of America, may have violated
the Hague Convention.

DEFENSE ATTORNEY G   If Your Honor please, I never once spoke
hypothetically. Your Honor and the attorney for the
prosecution have spoken in terms of hypothesis and suppo-
sition, but I have never done so.

PRESIDENT   I only wanted to know if you were aware of that fact.

DEFENSE ATTORNEY G   Of course I am perfectly well aware of it.
Mr. President, the fundamental duty of a defense attorney
is to protect the rights of the accused without regard to
his own personal interests or those of his homeland. The
sickest patient, whether murderer or war criminal, needs
the doctor. That is our sole theory, standard, and point
of view.

PRESIDENT   I do not intend to listen to a lecture on the theories,
standards, and points of view of a defense attorney at this
time, in this courtroom.

DEFENSE ATTORNEY G   Mr. President, I was not lecturing. I made
that statement to protect my right to speak without the
court's undue interference.

PRESIDENT   Will the attorney for the defense repeat that, please.
I was reading a note from a colleague.

DEFENSE ATTORNEY G   I objected to the court's undue interference with the defense's right to speak.

PRESIDENT   Mr. Attorney for the Defense—

DEFENSE ATTORNEY G   Mr. President, my homeland has violated the Hague Convention, and it is a very clear case of interference with my rights as counsel for you, Mr. President, even to suggest that I have turned that fact into a "questionable hypothesis" and am trying to make a deal with it.

PRESIDENT   Mr. Attorney for the Defense, you will use respectful terms here. You will not speak of undue interference by the court. You will withdraw that or you will leave this court as counsel. And you will apologize.

DEFENSE ATTORNEY G   I would like to explain to the court that I have been trying cases for twenty years and that the expression "undue interference" is not unusual—

PRESIDENT   You will withdraw that offensive expression "undue interference by the court." I will not listen to another word from you until you do. And you will apologize for using that expression. If you fail to do so, I shall submit to my colleagues that they cancel your authority to appear for the accused. You can always submit that the court should allow counsel to proceed as he proposes, but you are not authorized to use offensive expressions to the court in making your submissions. That is the difference.

DEFENSE ATTORNEY G   I had no intention of offending the court or of using offensive language, and I do not understand the nature of the impertinence to which Your Honor refers. In Australia, would such an expression be taken as contempt of court? In the United States of America—

PRESIDENT   That expression is indeed contemptuous of this court. I ask you again to withdraw the offensive expression "undue interference by the court."

DEFENSE ATTORNEY G   Well, I decline to do that, Your Honor.

DEFENSE ATTORNEY F   Your Honor—

PRESIDENT   The court will be recessed briefly, during which time I shall consider counsel's contempt of court and also the evidence concerning the atomic bomb. I have not yet had time to read the notes from my colleagues on that subject.

PROSECUTING ATTORNEY C Your Honor—

DEFENSE ATTORNEY F Your Honor, if you please. It is true that my colleague and I are representing and defending different defendants, but you must take note of the fact that both of us have had to disregard the interests of our own country in order to represent those of Japan. The particular expression my colleague used was inappropriate, but his general argument derives from a position which you surely agree with: namely, that the two atomic bombs dropped on Japan brought about an immediate termination of the war within a week.

PROSECUTING ATTORNEY C Your Honor, I object.

PRESIDENT I forgot that the Soviet attorney for the prosecution had asked for the floor.

PROSECUTING ATTORNEY C I object to the defense's statement that America's use of the bombs brought about a termination of the war. Through their statements, the American counsel are in fact attempting to dispose of historical facts unilaterally, to criticize these facts unobjectively, and to make counter-charges against the Allied Powers and against the Union of Soviet Socialist Republics in particular in regard to the actions we took against Japan as the aggressor in order to ensure world peace.

DEFENSE ATTORNEY F Your Honor, the defense is at a loss to understand this. Why has the Soviet attorney for the prosecution attacked us with such vehemence?

PRESIDENT Mr. Attorney for the Prosecution, I do not quite understand your intentions. Do you mean your present statement to be an objection?

PROSECUTING ATTORNEY C If Your Honor please, in order to fulfill its duty as an ally of the U.S.A. and Great Britian, the Soviet Union declared war against the Japanese aggressor on the 8th of August, 1945. Our purpose was to make Japan surrender unconditionally and to ensure general peace. We achieved our purpose.

DEFENSE ATTORNEY F It seems the Soviet attorney for the prosecution has pushed the debate ahead to the Soviet stage. It is very clear that the Soviet Union broke the Treaty of

Non-Aggression signed by the Soviet Union and Japan when it declared war, and the defense is fully prepared to submit evidence as proof of that fact when the proper time to do so has come.

PROSECUTING ATTORNEY C   There is no need for the Soviet Union to give further evidence of the legitimacy of that declaration of war. We already tendered ample evidence of that fact, and if the defense opens debate on this point again later in the trial, we shall soundly refute them at that time. I am speaking now in regard to the cowardly argument of the American attorney for the defense, who claims that the war was terminated by America's use of the atomic bomb. It must be remembered that the Soviet Union entered this war *only* at the request of the United States and England. At the Teheran Conference, two years before the termination of the war, the Soviet Union made a positive response to that request, despite the fact that we were then engaged in our bitter struggle with Nazi Germany. During those two succeeding years, we laid out plans and, as promised, on the 8th of August, 1945, the Soviet Union declared war on Japan and brought about a termination of the war.

PROSECUTING ATTORNEY B   Mr. President, as the American attorney for the defense has said, this is not the proper time to carry on this debate.

DEFENSE ATTORNEY F   When my statement is called a cowardly argument, I have no choice but to continue with it.

PRESIDENT   I remind both the attorneys that this court is an international tribunal. It should not be, it cannot afford to be colored by the slightest reference to international politics.

DEFENSE ATTORNEY F   I apologize if my statement sounded emotional. My only intention was to add a note of reason to the Soviet attorney's emotional outburst, for the fact of the matter is that the Americans were the first to develop the bomb, which they used effectively to bring about a quick termination of the war. As a result, countless numbers of lives in the belligerent nations were saved.

PROSECUTING ATTORNEY C   Is my argument founded any less on reason or on fact? The fact, for example, that the American President Truman for some reason did not reveal the creation of the atomic bomb to the Soviet Union at the Potsdam Conference. Or the fact that it dropped its new bomb over Hiroshima on August 6, 1945, a mere four days after the Potsdam Conference ended.

DEFENSE ATTORNEY G   Your Honor, I would like the court to strike this rash statement by the Soviet attorney from the record. Furthermore, the dropping of the bomb on the 6th of August in no way justifies the Soviet Union's act of the 8th of August—breaking the Treaty of Non-Aggression by declaring war on Japan.

PROSECUTING ATTORNEY C   As I said just now, the Soviet Union had long before agreed—or rather, had been made to agree—on that date as the day it would declare war on Japan.

DEFENSE ATTORNEY G   It is by now a well-known fact that the Soviet Union was thrown into confusion by the dropping of the bomb and precipitously declared war two days later.

PROSECUTING ATTORNEY C   It seems the attorney for the defense does not comprehend the word "fact." The so-called facts which he speaks of are nothing more than vicious and false rumors which have been circulated throughout the world. The facts I speak of are founded on truth. For example—

PRESIDENT   The Soviet attorney—

PROSECUTING ATTORNEY C   For example, I am able to report straight from the record the following statement made by the American Secretary of State Byrnes at Potsdam to high-ranking American military officers: "The task which we must carry out now is not to make the world safe for democracy, but to make the world safe for America."

DEFENSE ATTORNEY G   If the court please, this statement by the Soviet attorney is a vicious slander of my homeland and an unwarranted insult to a member nation of the Allies.

PRESIDENT   Please do not make me repeat this again. I will not see this international tribunal dragged into the whirlpool of international politics. The dispute is ended here.

DEFENSE ATTORNEY G   If Your Honor please—

PRESIDENT   This dispute is ended. We shall return to the point under consideration. Will the attorney for the defense withdraw the contemptuous expression "undue interference by the court"?

DEFENSE ATTORNEY G   I decline to do that, Your Honor.

PRESIDENT   The court is recessed briefly. During that time, I shall consider counsel's contempt of court and the evidence concerning the bomb tendered by the defense.

DEFENSE ATTORNEY H   Your Honor—

PRESIDENT   I will not hear anyone at all until the hearing has been resumed.

The entire stage is darkened and then lit again.

MARSHAL   The International Military Tribunal for the Far East is now resumed.

PRESIDENT   By majority the court rejects Defense Document No. 553, purporting to be an excerpt from the *Nippon Times* relating to the atomic bomb decision and to alleged observations by Mr. Stimson. The document will be marked for identification only.

CLERK   I repeat, Defense Document No. 553 will be given exhibit No. 2332 for identification only.

DEFENSE ATTORNEY H   Your Honor—

PRESIDENT   Next, in regard to the American attorney for the defense, by majority the court rules that he will henceforth be excluded from the trial for contempt of court.

DEFENSE ATTORNEY H   Your Honor—

PRESIDENT   The Japanese attorney for the defense has not been given the floor. The American counsel is excluded from these proceedings under this condition, that he will be allowed to return once he has satisfactorily withdrawn his contemptuous statement about this court and has apologized.

DEFENSE ATTORNEY G   I have no intention of changing my position and see no reason to change it, so I will assume I have been permanently excluded from this court. However, I believe that no one has the right to prevent me from sitting in the spectators' gallery and continuing to observe this trial. [*exits*]

PRESIDENT   The court is adjourned until 9:30 A.M. tomorrow—

DEFENSE ATTORNEY H   Your Honor—

PRESIDENT   What is it?

DEFENSE ATTORNEY H   I know that today is not my turn to speak, nor do I have any intention of entering into the present argument between the American attorney and the Soviet attorney about the atomic bomb. It terrifies me just to utter those words. But—

PRESIDENT   What is the purpose of your statement?

DEFENSE ATTORNEY H   My purpose? My statement has no purpose which could be found in courtroom procedures. I am speaking about my feelings.

PRESIDENT   The courtroom is not the place to speak about your feelings.

DEFENSE ATTORNEY H   I know that very well, but there is one thing I would like to say. Already, in February of last year, the year after the blast, the number of dead and wounded in Hiroshima alone was 129,000 people. That is a figure published by the American General Headquarters. Since then that number has been increasing.

DEFENSE ATTORNEY F   May I remind Your Honor that you have already declared the court to be recessed.

DEFENSE ATTORNEY H   And then, if you include the number from Nagasaki, the total number of victims of the atomic bomb is several hundred thousand. I was only wondering if—

PROSECUTING ATTORNEY C   If Your Honor please, I ask that you preserve the order of the court with all due severity.

DEFENSE ATTORNEY H   I was only wondering if the American attorney for the defense and the Soviet attorney for the prosecution have ever given any consideration to the tragic fate of those victims.

PRESIDENT   The courtroom is not the proper place for making speeches.

DEFENSE ATTORNEY H   This is not a speech. This is my— my—

PRESIDENT   Your feelings have no relevance to this court. On the first day this court began its proceedings, we stated that our duty was to preserve an open and fair attitude for both the facts and the law. The court is adjourned until 9:30 A.M. tomorrow.

End of Act III

Part II   Summer: A Romance of the South Seas

Act I

CHARACTERS

Tobosuke (a comedienne on the *manzai* stage)
The boy
Man A (formerly a private superior first-class in the Japanese
   Army)
Man B (formerly a private first-class in the Japanese Army)
Man C (formerly a private first-class in the Japanese Army)

A park, on an afternoon in late summer some years after the war.
The surroundings are still strewn with rubble from the bombing.
In the park are a rickety bench, a slide, swings, a jungle gym, and
several trees.
Tobosuke is trying to take a picture of the boy.

TOBOSUKE   Something's wrong. I still can't get you in focus.
BOY   Why not? I told you how to do it.
TOBOSUKE   Don't move.
BOY   I'm not moving. Can you see me in two places in the lens?
     All you have to do is twist it until the two are one.
TOBOSUKE   It's not working. I keep twisting it, but your face
     just won't line up.
BOY   Come on! That's a good camera. There aren't many people
     who've got one like it. Here, give me the camera, and you
     stand over there.
TOBOSUKE   Are you going to take my picture?
BOY   Look, nothing's wrong. You're in focus! Smile!
TOBOSUKE   Don't!
BOY   Why not?
TOBOSUKE   Just because!
BOY   I will anyway. [*He snaps the shutter.*] You went and moved.
TOBOSUKE   I'm no good either way, am I?
BOY   What do you mean?
TOBOSUKE   I can't take a picture, and no one can take one of me.
BOY   Something's funny.
TOBOSUKE   Well, I should think so.
BOY   Will you take my picture when it's not?
TOBOSUKE   [*with a smile, imitates the boy*] Will you take my picture
     when I'm not?
BOY   I will. When will you come here again?
TOBOSUKE   Well, I don't know. When will you come here again?
BOY   I usually come here every day. Goodbye. [*exits*]
TOBOSUKE   Goodbye.

     Man A enters.

TOBOSUKE   [*surprised*] Oh! What are you doing here?

MAN A   That's what I want to ask you. What are *you* doing here?
I mean, it's not hard to imagine why *I'd* be here. You're
pretty good friends, arent' you, you and the boy?

TOBOSUKE   Were you watching us the whole time?

MAN A   Do you know who the boy is?

TOBOSUKE   I know.

MAN A   You know? But do you know whose boy he is?

TOBOSUKE   I know.

MAN A   Well, if you know, why are you hanging around him?

TOBOSUKE   Stop it. What on earth would people think if they
heard you talking like that?

MAN A   And what do you think I think?

TOBOSUKE   What is that supposed to mean?

MAN A   How long have you been acquainted with the boy?

TOBOSUKE   Oh, from the time I was acquainted with him. Before
that, I didn't know him.

MAN A   Stop joking!

TOBOSUKE   Who's joking? Look at it this way. I knew him before
I knew him.

MAN A   What?

TOBOSUKE   Boy, are you dumb! Look, we became friends at some
point. I don't remember when. But I learned who he was
only after that. Now do you understand? I knew the boy
before I knew him.

MAN A   Of course! Which means that you knew him—no, that
is, the fact that you knew—no, let's see—you knew the
boy, right? Now, how long have you known him that way?
I mean, the way you knew him before you knew who he
was?

TOBOSUKE   Say, you'd be a natural for the trade. I mean, you've
really got a knack for it. Why don't we make a team?

MAN A   A team?

TOBOSUKE   On the *manzai* stage, of course. I dont' have a good
partner right now, and I need one badly.

MAN A   Quit changing the topic, will you? How long have you
known the boy?

TOBOSUKE   Persistent, aren't you? Well, I started coming here a
long time ago, just to sit on the bench sometimes and think
about nothing.

MAN A [*with a grunt of suspicion*] But why here? What brings you here?

TOBOSUKE [*affects a lisp*] I'm sorry, but I am unable to provide any information regarding that question.

MAN A Look, I'm serious.

TOBOSUKE So am I.

pause

MAN A His mother's house—the boy's mother—her house is right next to this park.

TOBOSUKE Which is why he comes here to play, I suppose.

MAN A And your house isn't by this park, is it? — Is it? — Well, have you met the lady?

TOBOSUKE The lady? That won't do now, will it. "His mother."

MAN A All right, then, his mother. And you've met her, haven't you?

TOBOSUKE What makes you so eager to know if I've ever met the boy's mother or not?

MAN A No, I meant—I mean, it doesn't really matter. I was just asking whether you'd ever met her, that's all.

TOBOSUKE [*angrily*] Why should I have? Why should I meet with her now, after all this time? What if I did meet with her? I wouldn't have a thing to say! No! What if I did meet with her and said something, anything? Do you know what would happen? We'd just be opening up each other's old wounds, that's all. You know I loved her husband once, and I can't think of any reason why she'd want to meet me now, any more than I'd want to meet her. Why should she? The lady, as you call her, has her son; she's made her entire life around him.

MAN A Hey, what are you getting so touchy for? I was surprised to find you and the boy here together. I was just asking, that's all. But why *do* you come here? You've been here more than once. You said so yourself, didn't you? Why?

pause

TOBOSUKE You stopped by there just now, didn't you? By the lady's house.

MAN A   I'm on my way there now. I'm waiting here for the rest of the group.

TOBOSUKE   Do you go there often?

MAN A   We go there from time to time, all of us together.

TOBOSUKE   What a lucky lady she is!

MAN A   Why?

TOBOSUKE   Why, to have men drop by like that all the time.

MAN A   But you should know we go there only because it's our duty, for all of us to go and console the survivors [*catches himself*]—the—the families of the men from our group.

TOBOSUKE   [*whistles*]   That was a very bad slip, wasn't it? The survivors, you said?

MAN A   No, I didn't say that. I said the families.

TOBOSUKE   So, consoling the survivors. You said it's your duty?

MAN A   Well, it is our duty, isn't it? Anyone who came back to Japan in one piece has got to, hasn't he? Sure, we don't go there *just* because it's our duty, but, look, at least we came back alive. This business, you know, of consoling the families of men who haven't come back yet; it's—it's not really our duty, it's more like our responsibility. Right?— What are you so quiet about?

TOBOSUKE   It must be awful work, running around to all those homes, consoling all those families of men who haven't come back yet. All that just for the sake of duty—sorry —responsibility.

MAN A   Well, we don't really go to everyone's home, you know. After all, I mean, it's hardly for us to go visit the wife of a major-general or a colonel.

TOBOSUKE   And the woman you're going to see? She has enough to buy her child a camera now, when no one else can afford one.

MAN A   He and I were together in the army, and he was the only one in the whole brigade who had graduated from college. So she could have been a lieutenant's wife at least, if he had just hung around the right people. All he had to do was take the cadet's exam, but he never did. He never did better than private, to the very end. I wonder why.

TOBOSUKE   Didn't you ever ask him?

MAN A   Sure I did. And I told him what I thought, too. That it was a waste for him to spend his time as a private. After all, he'd graduated from a good school.

TOBOSUKE And what did he say?

MAN A Nothing! He didn't say anything. He just smiled every time.

TOBOSUKE Really? He just smiled?

MAN A Maybe you know why. I'll bet you do. If anyone should know, it's you.

TOBOSUKE Did you ever try asking his wife?

MAN A Yes, I did.

TOBOSUKE What did she say?

MAN A Well, she didn't have any idea why either. Sometimes, she said, she wondered if he had gotten into trouble when he was a student and had a record that was holding him back. What did he do when he was a student?

TOBOSUKE I don't have any idea.

MAN A Really? Come on, I'll bet you do.

TOBOSUKE Maybe I should do the same—just say nothing and smile.

MAN A What are you talking about? Look, you're the only one who should know about him, right? And I'm the only one who knows that you're the only one who should know.

TOBOSUKE And what makes you think you can say that?

MAN A Because I know, that's why.

TOBOSUKE You're a fool. [*suddenly changes to a declamatory style*]

Our love is true!
The two avow
In warm embrace.
Yet shadows graze their hearts
As cherry blossoms scatter restlessly.

A spray of stars across the purple twilight sky.
A burst of wind-blown petals on a field of green.
Spring! Oh, Spring!
A romance of the Southern Seas in Spring.

This concludes the last act of "The Judge from the South Seas." [*returns to her normal voice*] He said he wouldn't be a miltary cadet. He said he would go on as a simple soldier to the end. He made the point very clear the day before he left.

MAN A   Where?

TOBOSUKE   Where what?

MAN A   Where did he say that to you?

TOBOSUKE   Here.

MAN A   Here?

TOBOSUKE   Here—right here where I'm sitting. There was a bench here that night too, but it was only a board placed across two big rocks.

MAN A   That night?

TOBOSUKE   In case you have the wrong idea, we sat here and talked, that's all.

MAN A   But she—the wife—was already around by then. I mean, he was already married by then, wasn't he?

TOBOSUKE   You're a natural, you know that? You'd be great up on the stage with me. You'd be perfect as my straight man. Shall I tell you why? Listen! First of all, if he hadn't been married by then, the wife could hardly be a depressed war widow now, could she? You're a natural! And second, she wouldn't have to put up with the ragtag bunch of you hanging around her, calling yourselves his war buddies. You're a natural! And just how old do you think that boy is? You natural. And then—ah, who cares! It doesn't matter, any of it. And just in case you have the wrong idea about our RE-LA-TION-SHIP—his and mine, you know?—I was the performer, and he was the patron. I was on the stage, and he was in the audience. And that is all there was to it.

MAN A   [*with a whistle of admiration and disbelief*]   That's a real act you've got. You're sure in the right business. When I said he was already married, I didn't mean it that way. I was simply asking you if you knew, at that time, that he was already married. You don't have to get so worked up.

TOBOSUKE   Worked up? About what? Look, that night, when my performance was over, he suddenly came to the green room door and told me his draft notice had finally come and that he wanted to talk to me.

MAN A   So you must have known him before that.

TOBOSUKE   Oh, I knew him all right. I'd catch sight of him every so often from the stage, and I'm sure he must have seen me quite a bit. That's what he came to the theater for. Anyway, that was when only three vaudeville halls were left. Everything else had burned down by then. We were all pretty desperate.

MAN A   And then?

TOBOSUKE   Well, we walked here from the theater.

MAN A   And then?

TOBOSUKE   The air raid sirens started up as we were walking here.

MAN A   And then?

TOBOSUKE   You're just like a cop, you know. When we got here, the raid began.

MAN A   And then?

TOBOSUKE   Then—we just sat here quietly, alone, and I remember him saying that it wouldn't matter too much if an incendiary bomb fell on us.

MAN A   Always the performer! There she is, with her stage set and waiting. Look, when I told you not to get so worked up, I meant that I already knew about you. He told me when he gave me the letter for you that he had been seeing you before he'd ever met his wife.

TOBOSUKE   I never saw him again after he married the mother of his child. I hope you heard that from him too.

MAN A   Well, he did say that he was forced to get married in a hurry.

TOBOSUKE   That's just my nature. I always step aside when someone I'm seeing gets engaged, whatever my feelings may be. That one night was different, though, when the two of us were sitting here, in the midst of the air raid. Everything I said before was true, really. After he got married, I was always on stage, and he was always in the audience. But I'm still waiting for him to come back, not that it would make much difference if he did.

MAN A   If you're using lines like that on stage, forget it. Who'd pay to hear that?

TOBOSUKE   [*after a pause*]   You know—

MAN A   What?

TOBOSUKE   They're going to hang him, no matter what. So why do they keep putting it off like this?

MAN A   What those people are doing is like an act of God. No one can figure out the will of God, can they? Well, that's just the way their president works. All he had to do was give the word, and death sentences were commuted to life imprisonment, and the men were sent back to Japan. Sure, everyone says that was all because a group of priests went there and made a big fuss, but so what? So what if the president did extend a pardon? What about the men who were hanged before the pardon? What does that mean for them? That they were unlucky? Are we supposed to write them off just like that?

TOBOSUKE   All the more power to anyone who can. What I want—what I'm hoping for more than anything else is part of what I hope for least of all.

MAN A   What does that riddle mean?

TOBOSUKE   You said God? Well, I suppose God must find it amusing to look down on us from on high. I mean, why not? Well, look at what I want! For that man to be spared and to come back, no matter what else. Well, now, supposing God hears me and sends him back. What happens? Why, he comes back only to become a complete stranger to me. Do you see what I mean? I mean, I can speak with him now all I want because he's beyond our reach. If he comes back, he's someone else's husband. But even so, I still hope that he comes back. What I'm hoping for most of all is part of what I hope for least of all. What should I do? If only I weren't like this, I'd be an awful lot happier, but I am like this, and I don't think even God himself could ever change me.

MAN A   But that's the way you are. That's how you think.

TOBOSUKE   It's enough to have that left in me, to see it in me clearly. I'm satisfied with that.

MAN A   That?—Oh, that!

TOBOSUKE   Yes, *that*, and stop looking as if you understood. [*declaims*] "A spray of stars across a purple twilight sky." [*breaks*] That's all I do, you know—brood about things while I recite my lines. What else can I do?

MAN A   Form a group to visit the survivors? March on their

prisons? You know, there's a singer who actually went and did that. And then she began a movement to petition for clemency. But I think it's too late now. Yes, it's much too late now.

TOBOSUKE   Ah, I want to be free of all this, to start out all over again, to live a new life. It's because of him, because he's still half-alive, that I suffer like this.

MAN A   Hey, what do you think you're saying! You say that now, but imagine you've heard he's really been executed. Imagine what you'll be thinking then. How do you think we'll both feel then?— I can't stand it, I can't stand even to think about it.

TOBOSUKE   Yes, let them execute him soon. Let them execute him soon. Let them hang him right away.

MAN A   Stop it!

TOBOSUKE   Quiet! I'm persuading myself. I'm trying to convince myself with words. Words are my trade, and if I can't convince myself, how can I ever say anything before anyone else? And don't you put *manzai* down either. The only people who get put down are those who ask for it. There was a war, and so we entertained the troops. That was called our patriotic duty. And then, and then when the Americans came, we changed the show. We started using broken English. It was enough to get a laugh. But that's not all there is to it, not for *manzai*, not even for *manzai*! [*suddenly deflated*] He taught me all that. Every one of those thoughts was planted in me by him. I guess that's why— well, that's not the only reason why, I know—let's face it, I'm not all that good—but that's partly why I'm not popular. But that's all right with me, because he planted that idea in me, of not being a popular success, and it pleases me not to be popular, so I'm happy. You know, if he just hadn't come to the green room door that last night, I might have forgotten all these things. I might have been able to forget. . . . Oh, he was a wicked man, coming to visit me at the green room—he didn't have to, you know— and then dragging me off to this park. We were no longer human, either of us, here, in the middle of that rain of incendiary bombs.

MAN A   In the middle of a rain of bombs. I know what you mean.

Like the time our little island was bombarded by battleships, and all that machine gun fire. I remember how it
was—just like being in the middle of a thunderstorm. No
sir, no one can stay human at a time like that, can they?

TOBOSUKE   No, they're like God.

MAN A   God?

TOBOSUKE   Yes, I was like God then. And so was he.

MAN A   Like God? No, I was an animal in the middle of a storm
of shells and machine gun fire. . . . We all had a bad time
of it. And that was the start of it all, wasn't it?

TOBOSUKE   The start? The start of what?

MAN A   The start of—of things, of everything.

TOBOSUKE   What do you mean, of things, of everything, of *what*?

MAN A   I don't know, but asking me like that won't help, I just
don't know how to say it. Some things you just can't put
into words. At any rate, well, for one thing, we're human
now, both of us, not animals, not God. Right? And we
ought to be grateful.

TOBOSUKE   I don't understand a thing you're saying. What do
you mean, grateful? To whom?

MAN A   I don't know. No one in particular, I guess. Well, the war
has ended. Maybe we should be grateful to this world,
just the way it is. Agreed? [*He tries to embrace her.*]

TOBOSUKE   Stop it! What do you think you're doing?

MAN A   I want to clear something up right now. Do you remember? "I want to be free of all this." You meant it,
didn't you?

TOBOSUKE   Free?—Ah, yes, I do want to be free of all this.

MAN A   And then, after that, then you said you wanted to start
out all over again and live a new life, right?

TOBOSUKE   New life?—Ah, yes, I do, I want to live a new life.
[*Man A kisses Tobosuke.*] Stop it! People will look at us!

MAN A   They say it doesn't matter much anymore. Why, you can
go down to the plaza in front of the Emperor's palace, and
there's a crowd of young couples lying in the grass and
kissing, right in broad daylight.

TOBOSUKE   You should know that everything has its proper time
and place. Why, I had just finished talking about all my
romantic memories of this park, and all very seriously,

when you suddenly started talking like that! That's very imperceptive of you. You have no appreciation of the subtler points in life. You'd be a natural, you know that? You really would.

MAN A   That's fine with me. Why, you said so yourself a minute ago. Remember? You asked me to team up with you because you needed a natural.

TOBOSUKE   Let me teach you a bit of *manzai* wisdom. The partner you team up with is your enemy. Think about it, it makes sense. In the crossfire on stage, one person eats and the other gets eaten. You should visit a green room sometime.

MAN A   But some of the teams up on stage are married, aren't they?

TOBOSUKE   Yes, and it's a pretty sure thing that they'll end up separated.

MAN A   And what would I be doing with you? [*laughs*] I really swallowed the bait whole, didn't I? Don't get the wrong idea. I wasn't thinking of doing a *manzai* routine with you.

TOBOSUKE   I was so sure that you'd come to visit me now and then since you and he were in the army together. And not because you thought it was your duty, or your responsibility, either.

MAN A   Why should I? After all, it's not my duty or my responsibility to go looking you up.

TOBOSUKE   Please, stop! What else could I think? Since you'd bothered to find me and give me his letter in the first place, I was sure you'd come again.

MAN A   I—I've been thinking about these things for a while, but I never tried to speak about them before.

TOBOSUKE   I'm sorry for being so slow. I never said I disliked you.

MAN A   So I finally said it all to you, and what's come of it? Do you remember I told you once about coming back to Japan only to find my family had all died and my house burned down? I was all alone, but I kept thinking I'd find a way somehow to start up again, get my old business going. I think the same things as you—start out clean, start a new life. And then you—I couldn't help feeling—it's all thanks to him—that you came along, and you and I were meant for each other, and then I said it, I finally said it today, in so many words. [*He kisses her again.*]

TOBOSUKE I told you people would look, didn't I?

MAN A And I told you it doesn't matter. Besides, who'd waste his time watching two beggars like us?

Tobosuke suddenly exits.

MAN A She wasn't kidding. Someone was watching. But then, why shouldn't he? He came here to meet me.

Man B enters.

MAN A When did you get here?

MAN B Was I in the way just now?

MAN A Are you alone?

MAN B Hasn't he come yet?

MAN A You know damn well if he isn't early, he's always late. I've never known him to do anything on time in his life, not once since we met in the army.

MAN B Shall I take a walk somewhere?

MAN A Don't get the wrong idea about me and her. She's the one I delivered his letter to, that's all—the woman it took me so long to find.

MAN B His letter? Whose letter?

MAN A Who do you think? I'd hardly be delivering a letter for the man we're waiting for! Him! It's him, the one way back there where we came from.

MAN B [*in surprise*] You mean then that he—I mean, the private superior first-class—sent her, the woman here just now, that last letter?

MAN A That's right.

MAN B The private superior first-class? sent her, that woman? his last letter?

MAN A You don't have to get so excited about it.

MAN B No, I mean, it's just that I'm a bit surprised to hear it was his last letter.

MAN A Son of a bitch! You're the one who said it was his last, not me. Besides, what if he did graduate from college, he's still human, isn't he? Anyone condemned to death wants to write to a lot of people and say what's on his mind.

MAN B He had that much to say to her?

MAN A   No, no, I didn't mean it like that. People say what's on their minds, that's all. Look, why were you late?

MAN B   Well, actually [*suddenly, as if from habit, he lowers his voice*] I stopped by the Repatriates Relief Bureau on the way, and, I'm sorry to say, that made me a bit late. Ah, there he is! Hey, what kept you so long?

Man C enters.

MAN C   I swear, something always comes up, every time I try to keep to a schedule. It's been that way ever since I was in the army.

MAN B   And we've known that very well since then. What happened today?

MAN C   Well, you remember, it was my turn to buy something to give the wife when we visit today. The fact is, I forgot about it.

MAN B   It's amazing you even remembered that you forgot. What did you do when you remembered?

MAN C   Well, by then, there wasn't any time to pick something up on the black market.

MAN B   You mean you came empty-handed?

MAN C   Right.

MAN B   What do you mean, right!? Do you realize you never succeeded once, to the very end! You never got beyond private first-class, even after Potsdam. But then, I didn't either.

MAN A   [*lowering his voice, to Man B*]   Was there any news?

MAN C   [*also lowering his voice. The following scene should be played with the three men speaking with lowered voices, as if conferring on some secret. To Man A*]   What do you mean? [*He stares at Man B. Man B makes no response.*]

MAN A   [*to Man C*]   He stopped by the Relief Bureau on his way here.

MAN C   [*to Man B*]   Well, did you hear anything?

MAN B   As far as they know, no report about this [*makes a gesture with his hands of being hanged*] has come in yet, one way or the other.

MAN A   I wonder what they mean by waiting like this. How long do you think they're going to put it off?

MAN C   Do you think they're going to grant a general amnesty sometime soon?

MAN A   I don't see that happening, but no one can really say. The whole thing depends on their will, on God's will.

MAN B   God?

MAN A   [*reverting to his normal voice*]   Forget it. We can't do anything about it. Come on, let's go. Look, you two go on ahead. I'll be there in a few minutes.

MAN C   What's wrong?

MAN B   Sure, I see. Come on, let's go. [*Man B and Man C exit.*]

MAN A   Let them hang him right away! That's what she said. Let them hang him. That's an awful thing to say. But maybe she really meant it. I want to be free of all this. That's what she said. To be free, to start out all over again, to live a new life. And why not? No one can go on like this, dangling forever. Is that what you [*meaning himself*] really think you should do—let her be free of him? Do you really think you should? Do you? But look, really, there's no way he can be saved now anyway. Things have already gone this far, there's no way back now. But that's what I want too, to feel free now. Sure I do, but how can I ever tell her, put it to her? Should I say something simple today, drop a hint and leave her? Is that what I should do? I started to tell her just now anyway. But maybe I shouldn't. It's going to happen sooner or later anyway, but maybe—yes, that would be better, meet her when everything is finished, over. That way, she'd—What? You've come back!

Tobosuke enters.

TOBOSUKE   What are you doing, standing here, muttering to yourself? What's wrong? You look terrible.

MAN A   What's wrong? How do I look?

TOBOSUKE   Dreadful. What were you talking about, the three of you standing here whispering together? What do you mean, "when everything is over"?

MAN A   What?

TOBOSUKE   And what did that mean—his hands on his throat?

MAN A   Hands?

TOBOSUKE   Yes, his hands, the big man, with his hands on his throat. What was that?

MAN A   His hands? That—that . . . was . . . only—

TOBOSUKE   Tell me the truth! Oh! You're such a natural! Has he been hanged?

MAN A   Well, no, it's just that sooner or later, we know it will happen, don't we? I mean, that's just it—we all know it, so—I might as well tell you now.

TOBOSUKE   So it's . . . really . . . happened?

MAN A   No, it's—it's just that sooner or later he will be hanged. Sooner or later it's bound to happen, and then—what it really is, you're right, it's God's will.

Tobosuke makes no reply.

MAN A   Go home, okay? Go home and wait for me there. I'm going to his home to talk with his wife, and right after that, I'll stop by your place. I promise. [*exits*]

TOBOSUKE   Have they finally carried out his sentence? Death by hanging? Oh, I don't know, I don't know what to think at all. It's so utterly different from what I thought it would be. I'm not even sure who I am. I never thought I'd feel like this. I never even dreamed it. Everything's so different, it's changed, the very scene around me looks different somehow. [*to herself*] You were prepared, weren't you? You were ready, you had steeled yourself, hadn't you? And what happened? That self so full of resolve has gone off somewhere, and I am someone else. What should I do? God's will, he said? And what is God? Am I supposed to stand here doing nothing, obedient to some vague, unknowable will? To simply watch in silence? Listen, you! I don't care if you're God or who you are. I was in that rain of bombs, I was God once, too. You're not going to get by that easily. You're going to have to answer to me, you hear? You're going to have to! I don't know what to do. I haven't got the vaguest idea how to go about it, but I'll find something to do. That will give me time to figure it out. You watch! I'll never let you go without doing something! You watch! It won't take long, you hear! You goddam God!

The boy enters.

BOY   Are you still here?

TOBOSUKE   [*an exclamation of surprise, and then a pause*]   Come here.

BOY   Why?

TOBOSUKE   Just come here. [*The boy goes to her, and she hugs him tightly.*]

BOY   What's wrong with you? You look funny.

TOBOSUKE   Did those men say something?

BOY   What men?

TOBOSUKE   You know, the men who always come to your house. Did they say something?

BOY   I didn't see them.

TOBOSUKE   You didn't? Why not?

BOY   I was at the station.

TOBOSUKE   At the station?

BOY   I was waiting for my mother.

TOBOSUKE   Your mother isn't home?

BOY   No, she's out.

TOBOSUKE   And?

BOY   And what?

TOBOSUKE   What is your mother doing?

BOY   She's back now.

TOBOSUKE   Did you walk here together?

BOY   No, she was looking at the shops in front of the station. She wasn't buying anything, just looking, so I came here alone.

TOBOSUKE   Do you remember the air raids?

BOY   No, not at all.

TOBOSUKE   Really? Not at all? [*The boy begins to play on the slide and other equipment, and Tobosuke, either unaware or unconcerned, continues to talk to him.*] That's funny. All of a sudden I can't remember them either, and I was right in the middle of all those bombs when they were exploding. You know, an air raid is very pretty when you see it far away. It looks like fireworks—great, big sprays of sparks opening up slowly in the sky like flowers, and not a single sound. It was as if I were sitting right in the middle of them—not a single sound, right in the middle of the silence. Besides, I was here in the park, and there isn't very much that can burn here. And all the incendiary bombs came falling down here and there, and flames blazing up just like jack-o-lanterns, everywhere.

BOY There's my mom.

TOBOSUKE Yes, I really must meet your mother.

BOY My mom?

TOBOSUKE I decided to just now.

BOY What do you want to meet her for?

TOBOSUKE What for? Oh, for reasons, lots and lots of reasons, and I don't even know how to talk about them.

BOY You're strange, you know that?

TOBOSUKE You're right. I am strange, I really am, now.

BOY She's come back. [*He interrupts Tobosuke, who is about to speak.*] I'll get her. [*exits*]

TOBOSUKE What should I say when I meet her? I don't know, it seems as if there's so much to say, and nothing to say at all. But I have to meet her. He says so. He says I have to, I have to tell her everything, even the most unpleasant things, if I'm going to have my say with God. Yes, to have my say with God.

End of Act I

Act II

CHARACTERS

Tobosuke
Kiyoko
The boy
Man A
Man B
Man C

Tobosuke and Kiyoko are seated in the park.

TOBOSUKE   [*after a long silence*]   I—I guess I've told you everything now.

KIYOKO   [*also pauses*]   That's the third time.

TOBOSUKE   The third time?

KIYOKO   The third time you've said you've told me everything.

TOBOSUKE   Oh, I see, the third time. Was that the third? Well, you
see, I do talk an awful lot, and then, well, you've been silent
the whole time. That always makes me nervous, when people are silent, it makes me afraid there will be a lull, and
then God knows what might happen, and I simply feel I
must keep on talking. I guess it's a habit, but actually, it's
part of my profession. I'm sorry. [*pause*] But—please, won't
you say something? Really, now that I finally made up my
mind and told you all this, everything there was to tell, you
can't just keep silent. I feel so awkward. I mean, of course,
I understand that you must be very upset by this. After all,
there I was, a stranger, waiting for you here, of all places,
as if I were going to ambush you, and then suddenly telling
you all these absurd things. But I'm serious, really I am,
seriously serious about this. And everything I said to you
really was true, all of it. But why, when I didn't have anything to say, did I go ahead and say it all anyway? There,
that's the fourth time. No, it must be the fifth. [*pause*]
Please, say something, anything. I've finally told you
everything on my mind. Now you've got to give me a line
that I can exit on. Tell me you're angry, or surprised, or
that you never want to see me again.

KIYOKO   I've been thinking about something a bit different, about
the fact that I never heard a single thing about you from
him.

TOBOSUKE   Ah, from him. Yes, he said he never told you anything
about me. [*in confusion*] I mean there was nothing between
us. I told you that just now. He never said anything because
there was nothing between us to tell.

KIYOKO   Between whom? I suppose you can think of it that way,
"nothing between you." I suppose it seems so to you,

you're so proud of how you "stepped aside" in the whole affair.

TOBOSUKE   Proud? Do you think that's why I said there was nothing? Nothing? Let me tell you, there most certainly was something there. Do you think I would have told you these things now if there hadn't been?

KIYOKO   If you're going to be this angry, you should have said nothing from the outset. No one came and sought you out. You didn't need to talk on and on about these things, all by yourself.

TOBOSUKE   Do you mean to say you have no idea what feelings led me to tell you all that I did just now?

KIYOKO   But I'm certain you can imagine my feelings at least, being made to listen to what you said, my dear.

TOBOSUKE   Can I? My feelings are different. You see, I was never forced into a marriage at the last moment—the wife of a man who was going off to war and needed a woman as a formality to make certain his family line would keep going.

KIYOKO   I do not make a profession of talking. I am quite incapable of such glibness—or, I might add, of such vulgarity—but, I assure you, I have a great many feelings of my own, which is only reasonable, I'm sure you'll agree.

TOBOSUKE   Reasonable? Who's reasonable? I'm not, which is why I told you all that I did when I didn't have anything to tell. [*despondently*] But maybe it was wrong after all, to have said these things.

KIYOKO   Did you really ever think it was the right thing to do? Why, you said it yourself. There was no need to talk. And yet, when it wasn't right, when you didn't need to, you knew all that, and yet you told me everything, didn't you?

TOBOSUKE   Yes, I did.

KIYOKO   Why?

TOBOSUKE   Why did I do that? I'm not very good at theory. I'm sorry. But, you do understand, don't you?

KIYOKO   What am I supposed to understand? When you suddenly approach me—you yourself said it was like an ambush—when you practically pounce on me and suddenly begin telling me all these things about yourself and my husband,

and then to turn around and tell me I'm too silent! What could I possibly have said?

TOBOSUKE   That's true, it really is. I'm sorry.

KIYOKO   Sorry? It's too late for apologies, I would say, when you didn't need to say anything from the outset. All you needed to do was watch me walk by and think to yourself that one foolish woman who knew nothing at all was passing by. You were the one to begin this, this absurd affair, and it's up to you to find a way to end it.

TOBOSUKE   You are right, really, you are. I'm sorry.

KIYOKO   Let me tell you quite frankly that I have no desire at all to hear anything more about your feelings. I do not care what they are, and I feel no need or desire to hear you talk about them. I asked you before. The only thing I want to know is why you began speaking the way you did.

TOBOSUKE   I'd hoped you'd be angry with me, but angry in a different way somehow.

KIYOKO   Different way? How?

TOBOSUKE   Well, I told you I hoped you'd never want to see me again, remember? Something like that.

KIYOKO   Believe me, I have no intention of seeing you again, if you'd simply answer my question. What was it you wanted to say when you began talking to me like that?

TOBOSUKE   I don't know, but I hadn't planned on things turning out like this. Somehow it would have been better if we had parted company as we were before, furiously angry with each other.

KIYOKO   That's not so at all. Isn't that why you spoke as you did, because you wanted to tell me what I'm asking you now? Perhaps you didn't realize it, but I'm certain that's why. As I remember, this is what you people call a set-up, isn't it?

TOBOSUKE   Set-up? Ah, the set-up! Setting up the audience. You're right. Maybe that's what it was. Well, if it was, you know, it certainly took me a long time to set you up. The next act will be on before I even get to the story. Just like every other pathetic storyteller these days.

KIYOKO   But that's why the set-up worked—because it was long.

I wouldn't have realized what was happening if it hadn't been. Of course I was surprised, at first. I thought you were ridiculous. Of course I was angry. But I gradually realized that I'd wait until I heard from you what I wanted to hear. I'm not certain why, you know. You mustn't run off to your green room.

TOBOSUKE   My, it's cheered up a bit, hasn't it. You know, you seem different, completely different from the lady I had imagined you'd be.

KIYOKO   [*smiles*]   And what did you think I would be like?

TOBOSUKE   More—I don't know—much more typical, I guess. You know the kind I mean, you find them everywhere. I thought you would be like that. I'm sorry.

KIYOKO   Forced into a marriage at the last moment—the wife of a man going off to war who needed—

TOBOSUKE   No, no, no! I said that without thinking.

KIYOKO   —a woman as a formality to make certain his family line would keep going. That's exactly how it was. [*She talks down Tobosuke, who is about to say something.*] No, it was. That in fact is exactly how it was. We were forced to do it by the war. Only, after that, something unexpected happened.

TOBOSUKE   What was that?

KIYOKO   Oh, this present life of mine came after that—"the wife of a war criminal." I've been living it for years now, much longer than the time we spent living together. "Wife of a war criminal"—I wonder if you understand how miserable that is.

TOBOSUKE   Miserable? I could put up with a lot of misery. I've been poor ever since I was born.

KIYOKO   I meant something different, something you'd have to experience to understand. I mea thatn it is miserable to be known as a war criminal's wife, even if your husband hasn't committed a war crime. And it doesn't matter if a few people insist that no crime was committed, once the crime has been proved. His crime has already been proved, before the entire world.

TOBOSUKE   Proved? Who proved it?

KIYOKO   I don't know. God, perhaps.

TOBOSUKE   God? Oh yes, God. My God has certainly put in a good showing today.

KIYOKO   I've been told time and again how indiscriminate the sentences for B- and C-class defendants abroad were. I've been assured repeatedly that he was unjustly accused. Please, don't misunderstand me, it's been a comfort to be told these things. But even if I were told a million times, what good does it do, once his guilt has been proved, once he has been found guilty by God?

TOBOSUKE   [*pause*] You know, that's where you and I are different. In fact, that's what I plan to do—to defy God. And I guess that's why I came here and started talking to you.

KIYOKO   Defy God?

TOBOSUKE   Yes, defy God. I understand it a little now—why I did what I did—start talking to you like a fool. I'm not like you. I don't care who I'm facing, even if it's God. I'm not the one to surrender.

KIYOKO   Surrender?

TOBOSUKE   Isn't that what you've done—surrender? God has proved it, you say? Haven't you given up? God has proved it to the world! To the world? It's an utter exaggeration. If I were you, I wouldn't care if my husband were a thief, if I loved the man. I wouldn't care if the whole world called him a thief.

KIYOKO   But a thief is different from a war criminal.

TOBOSUKE   How? What do you mean, that one is on a low level and the other one high? Maybe, and maybe not, but I don't think that's what's really bothering you. I think all you're worried about is your reputation. A self-serving surrender. I despise people like you.

KIYOKO   I guess I'm not as clever as you. I don't understand why you've suddenly gotten so angry.

TOBOSUKE   You know why I'm angry? I'm angry because I'm stupid. Because I can't think of anything else to do except be angry! Because I'm not capable of giving up the way you have!

KIYOKO   You've certainly gone out of your way to tell me I've given up, but I've been as active as I can. I've done as much as I can in my own way—petition for clemency and all the rest.

TOBOSUKE No, no, no, that's not what I mean at all. To begin with, what good are petitions going to do him now? But—then—I suppose you haven't heard yet.

KIYOKO Heard what?

TOBOSUKE [*pause*] Those men—the soldiers who stood trial with him for war crimes—came by here a while ago.

KIYOKO Do you know them?

TOBOSUKE The three of them came by.

KIYOKO How do you know them?

TOBOSUKE I wonder if they'll be coming back this way soon, since you're not at home.

KIYOKO They'll probably go in and wait for me. Mother's at home. Did they tell you anything?

TOBOSUKE I really know only one of them, the one who takes himself so seriously. I believe he said they were together all the time from when they were inducted—he and your husband?

KIYOKO How did you know that? Yes, he told me the same thing.

TOBOSUKE You know, I just realized something—for the very first time. If the two of them were together the whole time, why was he the only one allowed to come back? Why was he the only one to come back alive, someone like him?

KIYOKO Did they say anything to you?

TOBOSUKE You'll learn about it sooner or later anyway. They said that—that—the sentence was carried out.

KIYOKO They told you that?

TOBOSUKE They told me that your husband—was hanged.

KIYOKO [*pause*] I see. . . . I suppose official notification will arrive soon enough, but if they were the ones who told you, it's probably true, isn't it? After all, they go down to the Relief Bureau and the Public Welfare Office every day.

TOBOSUKE [*pause*] You seem very calm, don't you?

KIYOKO [*angrily*] Calm? Who says I'm calm! I've spent a long, long time preparing myself, steeling myself for what would happen today. That's all.

TOBOSUKE [*pause*] Don't you think you ought to go home?

KIYOKO   If I haven't, it's because you've kept me here. Well, haven't you?

TOBOSUKE   [*pause*]   What do you plan to do now?

KIYOKO   That's what I wanted to ask you. I told you before that I've taken every possible means, done everything conceivable, and yet it all was in vain. Of course I don't want to think so until I receive some sort of formal notification in person. But if they told you so, what else can I think? No, it was all in vain. He's gone, and I must understand this to be true. That's why, for me, there is nothing more I can do. It's beyond hope of retrieval, isn't it?

TOBOSUKE   Beyond hope? That's what I intend to do, to retrieve the irretrievable. You know, while he was alive, I was such a fool. Really! Think of it, I did nothing at all. Why, it never even occurred to me to try to take some measure or other. I was simply lost in memories, I brooded over them. But now that it's settled, I must do something. I must have satisfaction.

KIYOKO   [*pause*]   You seem different, completely different, from the person I thought you were at first.

TOBOSUKE   What did you think I was like?

KIYOKO   I understand a bit more now too. You can see a world that is different from mine, from ours. What was it you said? You'd complain to God? No, you said you'd defy him, didn't you? You know, you strike me as a person who could do it, too.

TOBOSUKE   Really? Do you really think so? Do you really think that I can defy God?

KIYOKO   Your work seems to have begun somehow. You waited there in ambush for me, not even knowing why yourself, and then again, without knowing why, you said to me all those things that would best have been left unsaid. You yourself said so, didn't you? It's begun, I tell you, and whatever it is, you'll have no rest, you can't turn aside. I know, to put it in your words—the work of defying God.

TOBOSUKE   I know—my work—retrieve what is beyond hope of retrieval. It has begun. Yes, my work—defy God. But how can I do it? What should I do?

KIYOKO   That's why something will happen, isn't it, because you

don't know what to do? And when it happens, you're the
one to take it up and see that it gets done.

The boy enters.

BOY   Mom, what are you doing? Those men have come again.
They're getting ready to go because you're so late!
KIYOKO   Did they say something?
BOY   Something? What?
KIYOKO   When Grandmother was talking with them, how did she
look?
BOY   Look? She looked like Grandmother, the way she always
looks.
TOBOSUKE   [*to Kiyoko*]   They haven't said anything. They're not
capable of mentioning the subject.
KIYOKO   I suppose not. No, I'm sure you're right.
BOY   Mom, this lady couldn't take my picture. And when I
wanted to take hers, she said hers couldn't be taken either.
She's really funny.
KIYOKO   Well, what's wrong with that? Nowadays, it's people
who think they're not funny that really are!
BOY   [*startled*]   What's wrong, Mom?
TOBOSUKE   Come here, to me, just for a little. [*She hugs him tightly.*]
But why was he the only one allowed to come back? Why
was he the only one to come back alive, someone like him?
BOY   What's wrong? You look so funny.
KIYOKO   [*to Tobosuke*]   You certainly ask impossible questions,
don't you? No! You certainly are the one who can ask them.
BOY   You're funny too, all of you! Look, those men have come.
[*He runs to the slide and begins playing.*]

Man A, Man B, and Man C enter.

TOBOSUKE   [*in a coy tone, to Man A, who is puzzled to see Tobosuke
and Kiyoko together*]   Good afternoon, private.
MAN A   [*embarrassed*]   Hello.
TOBOSUKE   What's wrong? You look upset.
MAN A   [*to Kiyoko*]   I'm sorry. I—we knew you were here, your
boy told us. But somehow we thought you'd be coming

back, and so we waited there as long as we did. Your mother
didn't seem to want us to go, either. We just were able
to get away now, when we told her we'd have to be leaving
for today. . . . Hey, just a minute. [*He takes Tobosuke off
to the side.*] What have you been talking about?

TOBOSUKE   I've got something I want to ask you, too.

MAN A   I hope you haven't said anything to her about it yet, you
know, about him—her husband. You haven't, have you?

TOBOSUKE   Why not? After all, you were going to tell her, weren't
you?

MAN A   Fool! There's a proper time for everything! And there's a
right way of doing things, too! Did you really tell her?

TOBOSUKE   I told you there's something I want to ask you.

MAN A   If you don't answer me, I'm telling you, I'll tell her everything about you and him.

TOBOSUKE   Him? You mean her husband? You'll tell her? [*laughs*]
I'm sorry, but I've already told her everything.

MAN A   What!

KIYOKO   [*to Man A*]   You're very troubled, aren't you, trying to
find some way to tell me, but I've already heard everything
from her. You don't need to say anything, if that report
was true.

MAN A   Well, what the hell! There's nothing left for us to say, I
guess. [*to Man B and Man C*] Hey, come on, that's it for today. Let's go.

TOBOSUKE   Wait a minute.

MAN A   Look, ah, why don't I drop by your place, on my way
back, you know?

KIYOKO   I'm sorry, but I'd also like to have you wait for just a
minute. [*to Man A*] Not just you, all of you.

MAN A   Has something happened? If not, I've got some other
things to—

TOBOSUKE   It's not going to help you to try and escape. It's not
the proper time for those excuses, is it now?

MAN A   We're stuck, can't move! I feel just like I've been dragged
into that courtroom once again. What's going on? [*to Man
B and Man C*] Hey, you two, come over here, line up! Line
up together! Dress it up! Not that I have any idea what's
happened.

TOBOSUKE   Sorry, but we're the ones who don't know what happened. Tell me, why are you alive? And why did the dead
die?

MAN A   I don't—I don't know.

KIYOKO   But you all really must answer her, you know.

TOBOSUKE   Why did the dead die? And why are you alive?

MAN A   But, that—I mean—there were so many things—so many
reasons.

TOBOSUKE   [*sits on the swing, and as she begins to swing gently, she
speaks in a declamatory tone*]   "Offer thanks to those noble
spirits who have fallen in defense of the homeland!" That
was from "The People's Pledge." "We pray for the eternal
deliverance of His Majesty's soldiers and for certain victory
in the Greater East Asia War. Prayer begins!" And then,
remember, we'd hold our breath for two counts. "Prayer
ends!" Even the *manzai* comedians and the raconteurs
went out in gaiters to visit the farming villages and the
factories. We were practically in rags by that time. We'd
line up on the stages of those dreadful little shacks. "All
stand and face the direction of the Imperial Palace! Bow
to the Palace!" "Let us all rise and recite the Pledge of
Victory together. One, we pledge ourselves entirely to our
Lord the Emperor. Two, we pledge ourselves entirely to
the protection of our country." Oh, now what were they?
There were three more, weren't there? Five in all, five oaths
in the Pledge. [*suddenly*] Tell me, what were you doing at
that time?

MAN A   At that time? When do you mean?

TOBOSUKE   [*swings in wider arcs*]   I remember. "One, we pledge
ourselves entirely to our Lord the Emperor. Two, we pledge
ourselves entirely to the defense of our country. Three,
we pledge ourselves entirely to productive labor, to the
utmost extent of our power. Four, we pledge ourselves entirely to a clean and moral life. Five, we pledge oursleves
entirely to victory in this holy war."

MAN A   [*doubling with Tobosuke's recitation, which she carries on in a
flat incantatory tone*]   There were so many things—so many
reasons—but what I really remember is what happened in
that trial.

Man B and Man C nod in agreement.

MAN A   At that time, when I was on trial, in that hot, hot land, hot even for a hot land, on a hot afternoon that summer so hot that you couldn't even imagine it, I stood for hours in that murky cellar, waiting for them to reach a verdict.

The stage is darkened, with only the figure of Man A left illuminated.

End of Act II

Act III

CHARACTERS

Those who have already appeared in the previous acts:

Man A
Man B
Man C
Tobosuke
Kiyoko

Those who now appear for the first time:

A Japanese army brigadier general
A Japanese naval captain (section head in the civil administration)
A Japanese army lieutenant-colonel (staff officer)
A Japanese naval civilian employee
A Japanese army sergeant
Kanohara (a private superior first-class in the Japanese army, Kiyoko's husband)

The presiding judge (a foreigner, apparently of the rank of lieutenant-colonel)
Two associate judges (foreigners, apparently of the ranks of captain and lieutenant)
The prosecutor (a foreigner, apparently of the rank of major)
An interpreter (second-generation Japanese-American)
A lawyer (a Japanese P.O.W., formerly an officer in the military judiciary)
Foreign soldiers

Woman A, a native
Woman B, a native
A man, a native
A boy, a native

Man A, illuminated from the previous act, is found alone on stage. A foreign soldier, carrying an automatic pistol, appears and hangs a sign with the figure "7" around Man A's neck.

MAN A   In that hot, hot land, hot even for a hot land, on a hot afternoon in that summer so hot that you couldn't even imagine it, I stood for hours in that murky cellar, waiting for them to reach a verdict. At the top of these stairs, [*pointing at the steps going up the slide*] the courtroom. The courtroom where we've all been on trial for the past three days. Oh, sure, three days, but I'll tell you the truth, the tribunal convened for two hours in the morning, then took a recess, then two hours in the afternoon, then it adjourned for the day. And the same on the next day. And then today, two hours this morning. Two plus two plus two plus two plus two—a measly ten hours to try every soldier held in this prison. And now I'm finally waiting for the verdict on this miserable landing on the stairs. It's like some musty foxhole. Over there are the cells. There's a number of men still waiting in them. Up above us a group's getting sentenced right now. [*The sound of some unintelligible foreign language can be heard being spoken high up in the darkness over the stage.*] And so I'm waiting here. For my turn, you know. I'm smoking a cigarette, see. I'm smoking and trying to calm myself. No, what the hell am I talking about—smoking a cigarette! No, wait, this *is* a cigarette. I know it's a cigarette. The lawyer's started bringing them down to us from time to time lately. You can see I'm holding it in my hand, but I just can't get it to my mouth, my hand's trembling so badly. And even when I do, my throat's so dry I don't even know if I've inhaled or not. And on top of everything else, I'm hungry. I'm so hungry my stomach feels like it's going to have cramps. You know, I think I read something about this somewhere, I mean, about times like this, times just like this. Every damn thing you've ever done in your life, everything that ever happened to you, sort of flashes by all at once before your eyes. And that's not all! Look at me! Here I am, right, thinking to myself that these people are just about the shrewdest group I've ever seen. I mean, look, here they are making me feel like this, making me think like this, making me wait forever in this murky hole while they're getting ready to make a decision on me. I mean, they're going to drive me crazy by what they're doing, and they know it. Here I am thinking all this, and yet here I am looking at me thinking all this and seeing me very clearly. It doesn't matter. The worst they'll give me is a year, right? But then they're all saying they give three years just like that, just for having struck a P.O.W. And worse than that, a lot of the death sentences they've given out have been to the wrong people. No kidding, to the wrong people! They get the names and numbers mixed up, and they know they're doing it too. I just don't know what they'll give me until I've gotten there. Oh! Brigadier General, sir!

GENERAL   [*descending the stairs as if being pushed down them. The foreign soldiers below take him and push him on farther into the darkness.*]   The firing squad. [*The sound of a steel cell door being closed behind him can be heard in the darkness.*]

MAN A   Firing squad? For the general? That's awful! A firing squad! That's awful. But—but he was taking it all pretty calmly, wasn't he? A firing squad. But, I mean, what could you expect, I mean, he was the most responsible, he was on top of the command. I guess there's no way he could get out of it. He has to face the firing squad. After all, he was the highest rank here, he was the most responsible. He has to take responsibility. I mean, if he didn't, where would that leave us? Wait, I've got it! He's been given the firing squad, not hanging. Of course! That means he's been treated the way he should be, I mean, as a career soldier, right? After all, he's the only one who acted like one throughout the whole trial, wasn't he? He told them he was responsible for everything, that he was in charge of command here and would take all the responsibility. Who knows? They finished the trial in only ten hours in three days, but maybe they really were doing it seriously. I mean, maybe they took his word, even when it didn't seem like it. I don't know. The prosecutors were a bunch of monkeys. But who knows, maybe they really were serious. Maybe the judges were, too. [*The section head of the naval civil administration enters.*] Captain, sir! What was the decision, sir?

CAPTAIN　[*brought down the stairs*]　Seventy years!

MAN A　Seventy years? Did you say seventy?

CAPTAIN　You know, that means I'll be serving sentence until I'm well past a hundred years old. I don't suppose it can be helped, though, I mean, the fact that the general and I are looked on as the people responsible.

MAN A　Only the two of you? But what about the lieutenant-colonel? Why, we all know he was the one who was behind everything. What about him?

CAPTAIN　[*already pushed on into the darkness*]　He was given three years. [*sound of steel cell door being closed*]

MAN A　Three years? That's all? The lieutenant-colonel was given only three years? Oh, sir! Sir! Lieutenant-colonel, sir! [*The lieutenant-colonel, the army staff officer, is pushed down the stairs and goes on into the darkness in silence. The sound of a steel cell door being closed.*] What the hell! What the hell is that supposed to mean! Every single one of us knew what was going on. Look, just because the general was a nice old guy, the lieutenant-colonel thought he could get away with anything. He pushed his weight around whenever and wherever he wanted to. We weren't blind, you know. And all they gave him was three years? What the hell, they might as well have let him go free, for all that's worth. And then they go and give the captain seventy years? Why did they do that? What about me? Ah, there they are! There they finally are. [*Three men—the naval civilian employee, the army sergeant, and Kanohara—pass by in silence.*] Hey! Hey! What happened? The three of you? [*sound of cell doors being closed in the distance*] Hanging! Those three? Do—do you hear me!—Those three—they didn't have anything to do with it, they weren't responsible! What? Me? It's my turn? My turn has come—now? Yes sir. [*He begins to climb the stairs.*] Oh, these stairs. For the past three days, morning, afternoon, then morning, afternoon, then today, morning, and now, this very moment, makes it the sixth time up them. Funny, they seem to get steeper each time, don't they? I guess it's because I've only got one more time to go down. Step by step—got to watch it real carefully—got to take them one at a time, or I'll trip and fall. One more step. One more step. Remember? It flashes by, everything you've ever done in your life, everything that ever happened to you, all at once, before your eyes. [*He stumbles and falls downward into the darkness below the stairs. The stage lights are dimmed out.*]

The stage is lit again with different lights, in which the slide, the swing, and all the other equipment appear as things completely different from, unrelated to, their original shapes and functions. The new lighting must be designed in such a way that areas of light and dark can be moved about the stage as called for in the script.
The highest part of the slide is the height of the courtroom floor. A number of people are seated like monkeys in branches which approximate the height of the top of the slide. Three of these people are the presiding judge, in stage center, and the associate judges, to his right and left. Downstage left are the prosecutor and the interpreter. In addition to these five foreign military personnel, on stage left is the Japanese lawyer.
At stage right (approximately on top of the jungle gym) are the witnesses' seats.
As the scene progresses, all the characters from time to time, when not occupied with dialogue, play on the playground equipment nearest them.

PROSECUTOR   [*with impassioned gestures*]   What I, as prosecutor, wish to state clearly, is that—a fact obvious to whoever perceives it—the natives of this small South Seas island, the unenlightened natives of this island, meek by nature, unlettered, unaware indeed of the very existence of money, that these people could not possibly have had the intelligence to organize the large-scale spy ring which the defendants claim they had. And that, moreover, as the previous testimony so eloquently gave us cause to suspect, not a single shred of evidence can be discovered that would indicate these people did actually carry on spy activity. But the defendants did carry on their cruel tortures, and, having tortured two islanders to death, proceeded to create from whole cloth this alleged "large-scale spy ring" among the islanders and then went on in fact to "punish" another sixty-six of them. The defendants acted contrary to the laws of that very humanity to which they belong; they transgressed international law and custom; they violated the Articles of War. Gentlemen of the court, the events of this affair are utterly transparent at every step—

From among the spectators to the trial, who cannot be seen by the audience, a chorus of monkey-like chattering arises in support of the prosecutor. A large number of flashbulbs flash as photographs are taken.

PRESIDING JUDGE   [*hitting what serves as his table with a gavel*]   The spectators will be quiet.

The nine Japanese military personnel, those who have appeared in this act previously, plus Man B and Man C, are illuminated squatting on a lower level, divided into three groups.

MAN A   The next thing they said really shocked us: "We do not regard you as human beings." I always thought those people were supposed to be so much better than us Japanese! And that interpreter! I don't know where he learned his Japanese, but it was the queerest language I'd ever heard, the way he said everything so politely. He stood there telling us the Allies would treat us just like the Japanese had treated Allied P.O.W.s —if anyone complained, he'd kindly be shot immediately. And do you remember, the day after that was the day we were going to be repatriated by ship? We were just like a flock of chickens running around, when someone threw a net over us, and tough luck for those who got caught in the net. It was their tough luck, that was all. Look, they didn't even have a formal warrant for anyone's arrest. . . . Hey, what is this? [*He stares at an imaginary wall.*]

MAN B   They make us open our mouths wide, and then they

spit in them, or they make us stare straight into the midday sun and then whip us if we blink. Or the barbed wire! They make us stand for an hour at a time with the barbs right under our nostrils. You know, they really had to think to figure out that many ways of working us over. And they never seem to have enough at this prison. Day and night they keep coming back to work us over some more. They make us scrub the floor with toothbrushes. They make us eat cigarettes. They shove their fat cocks in our faces and make us suck them off. But the worst of all is when the guards come at midnight and raid the cells. Have you ever had anyone hit you as hard as he can three times in the solar plexus and start kicking you like mad when you fall? You're sure it's all over. It's getting late. I wonder if they're going to make another raid tonight.

MAN A   [*deciphering graffiti*]   "Someone's going to die, and it's either me or you."

SERGEANT   They put a rope around my neck and make me crawl on all fours and cut the grass. Oh, God, is that humiliating! All right, I say, I'll think of it as physical exercise. It *is* exercise, after all.

MAN A   Here. "Don't worry, brother, it's my turn to walk the rope."

MAN B   If you think that's humiliating, I heard of one man whose face was shoved into a latrine. Listen, I'm so weak from malnutrition, my only hope is to figure out how to move as little as possible.

MAN A   "Left, right, step by step—it's a dangerous game we play."

SERGEANT   You know, I can't help feeling it's strange; we've been through as much as we have, and no one's committed suicide yet. What a mystery human beings are, all of us.

MAN A   There, I've got it. "Someone's going to die, and it's either me or you." "Don't worry, brother, it's my turn to walk the rope." "Left, right, step by step—it's a dangerous game we play." "Fall with a thump and you're off to hell." Hmm. Someone must have written it on this wall before he was hanged.

*   *   *

MAN C   But everything we did was on orders from above, wasn't it? After all, we were trained to consider orders from above the same as orders from the Emperor himself. I think the only reason these people have dumped soldiers like us in this hole is because they don't understand how the Imperial Army operates. There wasn't anyone lower than us in the whole army.

KANOHARA   [*flying a paper airplane*]   That's what the word "perpetrator" means.

MAN C   Perpetrator?

KANOHARA   I don't know what war crimes the Allies have accused you of, but whatever they are, the fact remains that you and I are being held as perpetrators of war crimes, class C.

MAN C   Then what does that make the people who gave us the orders?

KANOHARA   Class B war criminals. They're being held over there. [*He points at the cell where the lieutenant-colonel sits in stony silence.*] Lieutenant-colonels are always a class above us, even when they're war criminals. He's not class C, he's class B. Right, Lieutenant-colonel, sir?

The lieutenant-colonel remains silent.

KANOHARA   You know this war crimes tribunal, the one we're to appear in soon, you know how it looks to me? Like a rope they've stretched out to make you walk, and the only person who gets saved is the one who can walk the rope and not fall. It's a dangerous game we play. Like this—left, right, step by step. And the only person who can walk a rope like that is a very special kind of acrobat.

MAN C   Exactly, an acrobat. But what about the clumsy ones, people like me, who are going to fall no matter what? I think we should take a flying leap.

KANOHARA   Commit suicide? It's funny, but there haven't been many suicides, even now. Oh, not that there haven't been attempts. I've heard stories from a number of P.O.W.s. One man, an army doctor, found it impossible to hang himself when everything like cord and belts was taken away from

him, so first he thought of biting off his tongue. As soon as
he had thought of that, he remembered a captain he had
once examined who had gone mad at a field hospital and
had tried to bite his tongue off. All he did was bite it a
little, and the thing immediately swelled up in his mouth
like a big rubber ball, and for a full week the poor man
lay in bed suffering from a high fever and intense pain.
At the end of the week, he was still very much alive. Well,
then, our doctor next thought he would try to fracture his
skull, but as a doctor he knew very well that falling head-
first onto the concrete floor from the height of a bed would
hardly kill him. So the doctor continued to think about
the problem, and then he suddenly remembered a very
interesting accident. During the war, he had apparently
seen a solider slip as he was trying to get down off a truck
and die of a dislocated neck. That, thought the doctor,
would be effective, so he devised a means by which he
thought he could dislocate his neck. He folded up his blanket,
put it at the base of a wall and used it to do a headstand.
Now this he did so that all the weight of his body came
down on his neck. He hoped to break his neck and sever
the spinal cord. But—

LIEUTENANT-COLONEL   Shut up!

KANOHARA   —aside from being painful, it had no effect. So then,
he considered suicide by self-induced apoplexy—a stroke
—of genius. They say he did something or other to disrupt
the mechanisms in the carotid artery that control the flow
of blood to the head and once again tried a headstand.
His ears began to roar, and then he put one hand over his
adam's apple and suddenly squeezed very tight. Everything began to grow dark before his eyes, and there, in the
darkness—it would take a doctor to think of this one—
countless pips of light that looked like intestinal bacteria
flashed before his eyes—

LIEUTENANT-COLONEL   Shut up! Shut up, will you!

KANOHARA   At that very second, he fell over, and when he came
to, he could hear from the next cell—they were in solitary—
the sound of someone hitting the wall, worried about all
the noise coming from his side. Ah, well, the one and only

successful attempt I've heard of was a man who split his
skull open with a water pipe filled with sand, then poked
out the arteries with a fork—not a knife, mind you, a table
fork—and finally strangled himself with a tent cord. He,
I heard, was successful. I also heard he was a lieutenant-
colonel, the former commandant of a P.O.W. camp. The
only problem was that it took him three hours to die.

LIEUTENANT-COLONEL   Shut up! Shut up! Shut up!

KANOHARA   I'm not making this up, sir. He was a lieutenant-
colonel in the army, sir, just like you.

*   *   *

CIVILIAN EMPLOYEE   Does it still hurt, Captain, sir?

CAPTAIN   [to the brigadier general)   General, sir, are you all right?

GENERAL   [to the civilian employee]   How are you?

CIVILIAN EMPLOYEE   Frankly, sir, I don't know if I forget that
I'm hungry because I hurt so much, or forget that I hurt
so much because I'm so hungry. [The three exchange ironic
smiles.]

*   *   *

MAN A   You mean you wrote that? "Left, right, step by step—
it's a dangerous game we play. Fall with a thump and you're
off to hell." I was sure someone condemned to death had
written that on the wall before he died.

KANOHARA   Who knows? Maybe both of us will be condemned.

MAN A   Son of a bitch! They haven't even begun the trials yet,
have they?

KANOHARA   That doesn't matter. The Japanese are already passing judgment on us, before the Allies have even begun.

MAN A   What are you talking about?

KANOHARA   It's true. Look, as soon as we were told about the
defeat by the battalion commander, we were put in a
P.O.W. camp, and a month later we were brought to this
prison because we were accused of war crimes, right?
During that month, the commanding officers met to draw
up strategy, for presenting our case if we were accused of

war crimes. Okay, at that time they came and told us to make sure we all had the same story. I agreed to it at the time, but do you know what, goddamn it! They had pretty much settled matters already, at that time!

MAN A   Settled matters? What are you talking about? It doesn't matter what our C.O.s decide, the verdict has got to be reached in this tribunal here, doesn't it?

KANOHARA   That's the trick, that's the rope we're walking, and it's a very dangerous business. You really learned that song, didn't you?

MAN A   Who could help it? I've been staring at that wall every day now, wondering if my turn was next.

KANOHARA   Well, I guess I should simply expect the worst, the way you do—I guess.

MAN A   [waiting] . . . what else?

KANOHARA   I was thinking of something else. Anyway, we've got to keep our eyes peeled, not let anything by that might be turned to our advantage.

MAN A   What do you mean? Do you think there's a chance we might be able to get out of this?

KANOHARA   That's why we're walking a rope, and it all depends on whether you and I can put on a good show or not, that's all . . . I guess.

MAN A   [waiting] . . . guess . . . what?

KANOHARA   Nothing, really.

MAN A   Come on, you don't have to beat around the bush. What are you getting at? What else is there?

KANOHARA   Well, the truth is, I was thinking about the problem of guilt.

MAN A   Guilt? Guilt? What's the problem? They brought us in because we're guilty, didn't they?

KANOHARA   Don't be a fool! No one goes around calling himself guilty. That's the problem with the Japanese, we all agree with the man on top. There's something cheap about that.

MAN A   You mean the Allies must have done things as bad as we did?

KANOHARA   Which means our lots are really the same, only they've convinced themselves they're God right now.

MAN A   I see.

KANOHARA But if we had won, we'd have done the same, I'm
    sure.

MAN A We would?

KANOHARA That is where guilt lies. [*He quickly climbs to the top
    of the jungle gym.*]

MAN A What did you say?

KIYOKO Did he really say that?

MAN A Say what?

KIYOKO That that is where guilt lies?

MAN A He certainly did.

> *Kanohara begins a monologue from the top of the jungle gym,
> holding a pistol in his hand now. At the same time Kiyoko and Man
> A proceed with the lines of their conversation (in fact, two separate
> monologues), which are to be spoken in between the lines of Kano-
> hara's monologue.*

KIYOKO Did he really say that? "That is where guilt lies."

MAN A You know, sometimes what he said was hard to under-
    stand.

KIYOKO Oh, yes, he was like that, hard to understand sometimes.

MAN A So often, he'd just talk on and on, to himself, it seemed.

KIYOKO And then, suddenly, there he'd be, bantering with you.

MAN A I don't know, I think somehow I understood what he was
    talking about.

KIYOKO Oh, I thought he was so strange.

MAN A And he never tried to impress anyone just because he had
    graduated from college.

KIYOKO Finally, today, I've begun to understand why he was
    that way.

MAN A He was an unusual person, whatever else.

KIYOKO He tried so hard to love me.

MAN A That's what he said. The problem with the Japanese is
    that they always agree with the man on top. He said there's
    something cheap about that.

KIYOKO And now I understand how he felt. He suffered.

MAN A He was always telling us not to be cheap or petty.

KIYOKO And if he ever came back, I know he'd try to love me all
    the more.

MAN A   That's why he never gave up.

KIYOKO   He took on the guilt—

MAN A   He took on the guilt for crimes committed by no one ever knew whom.

KIYOKO   He took on the guilt for crimes committed by no one ever knew whom.

MAN A   "That is where guilt lies."

KIYOKO   "That is where guilt lies."

MAN A   Even after the tribunal had passed sentence, he continued to complain to the judge.

KIYOKO   He always tried to carry out what he thought had to be done.

MAN A   And after that, I heard, he wrote a long appeal in English.

KIYOKO   Ah!

MAN A   He really wanted to come back alive, didn't he?

KIYOKO   He tried to carry things out, whatever the cost.

MAN A   Yes, he did. That's why he wrote that long letter in English.

KIYOKO   He sent it to the judge, didn't he?

MAN A   No, to someone even higher up.

KIYOKO   Ah!

MAN A   He sent it directly to the regional commander himself.

Kiyoko buries her face in her hands.

*   *   *

KANOHARA   [*speaking from on top of the jungle gym, his speech over-lapping the above lines of Kiyoko and Man A*]   To be hanged—to be hanged. As far as they're concerned, anyone will do, just as long as there is a criminal. But their logic applies to us as well. Besides—I didn't do anything personally, but I don't have any proof that I was totally innocent either, when I was in a situation where something had to be done. Isn't that so? Isn't it? Isn't that so? To be hanged—to be hanged. That, however, I prefer to think of as a personally selected means of committing suicide—a means of suicide chosen on my own initiative. That's the best way to get any satisfaction from this—and I now am satisfied by this idea. Isn't that so? Isn't it? Isn't that so? Ah, I feel dizzy. . . . My head is spinning. Look down there through the thickets of this hot, steaming jungle, down there, at the beach off in the distance—look at the soldiers, like ants. Lots and lots of soldiers, running back and forth, frantically digging trenches—frantically piling up sandbags. It doesn't look real, does it? Like something out of a dream. Look, there, something billowing up into the sky [*At some point he drops the pistol to the floor, which Tobosuke picks up.*]—above the soldiers milling about like ants—a mirage, billowing up above them. It's rushing down on me all at once—surrounding me. [*The sound of leaves and branches blowing wildly in the wind is heard.*] Hot—hot—hot summer— the restaurant in the department store—with my mother. Glasses clattering together, a clear, clear sound—sparkling silverware. I remember ice cream—the color of fresh cream—a beautiful color, the color of fresh cream. Stop it! Open your eyes, wide! Battleships! They're all gray— like a toy parade—so many of them—so many, many of them! What was it, a painting? No, it was a photo—in *Boys' Club Magazine*—that was it, in *Boys' Club Magazine*— in the summer—summer vacation—on a hot, hot summer day—ice cream. Ah, they're moving the cannons—they look like matchsticks. Wait, that's the main battery—it's a broadside volley. They're turning them again—the matchsticks are aimed this way. Look, ice cream. No, that's smoke—white smoke! A broadside volley.

The roar of shells exploding behind him is heard. He suddenly is flung from the jungle gym and falls to the ground. The lieutenant-colonel is standing over him; the sounds of the cannons roaring and the shells exploding are heard intermittently.

LIEUTENANT-COLONEL   Well, soldier, are you in the army or the navy? Speak up! Are you serving in the army or in the navy?

KANOHARA   I'm a private superior first-class in the army, sir.

LIEUTENANT-COLONEL   You damn fool! Do you think I'm so stupid I don't know that! If you're a soldier in the army, act like one! Do you think you'll get away with this, sitting on your butt in the jungle with these damn fool sailors? We're under siege! The whole island might be blown to bits any minute!

KANOHARA   But, sir, I'm not in the frontline divisions, I'm in the civil administration, sir. Their—our base is here, sir, in the jungle.

LIEUTENANT-COLONEL   You goddamn fool! All the rest of you come out here! Line up! [*The sergeant, the civilian employee, and Man A come out and line up with Kanohara.*] What are your duties in the civil administration?

SERGEANT   Our duty is to preserve order among the island population.

LIEUTENANT-COLONEL   Fool! Do you think that's the way an army sergeant answers? What are you, a naval civilian employee?

CIVILIAN EMPLOYEE   Yes sir!

LIEUTENANT-COLONEL   And what are your duties? Speak up?

CIVILIAN EMPLOYEE   I'm supposed to produce physical laborers, coolies, from among the island population, sir.

LIEUTENANT-COLONEL   Fool! And you?

KANOHARA   I'm supposed to prevent theft of supplies by the natives, sir.

LIEUTENANT-COLONEL   A bunch of fools if I ever saw one! And you?

MAN A   My duty is to uncover spy rings, sir.

LIEUTENANT-COLONEL   Fine! And do you think we have time to worry about every stolen chicken and filched bag of rice when we're under fire? And you, what are you worried about rounding up coolies to build an airstrip for? Japan doesn't have a single airplane left! Your immediate duty is to round up spies! Wipe out the spy rings! You are to bring in every person who is even the slightest bit suspicious and work on him until he confesses. If he resists, you can fry his nuts in oil for all I care, but make him confess. Do you understand? [*The navy captain appears. The lieutenant-colonel salutes.*]

CAPTAIN   Do you have anything to report to the general?

LIEUTENANT-COLONEL   Yes. I've finished inspecting the front lines.

CAPTAIN   You'd better hurry, the general is just about to go out and inspect the lines himself. [*The lieutenant-colonel does not move.*] You'd better hurry.

LIEUTENANT-COLONEL   Captain, sir, what's happening about the spy ring?

CAPTAIN   We're carrying out a thorough investigation at present.

LIEUTENANT-COLONEL   That, sir, is what you always say, but it won't do now, sir, we can't afford to waste time. We must have it carried out thoroughly, sir, with all due speed.

CAPTAIN   We arrested forty-five persons for the first round of interrogation and executed thirty-eight of them upon brigade command.

LIEUTENANT-COLONEL   When does the second round end?

CAPTAIN   We have already arrested twenty-five.

LIEUTENANT-COLONEL   When are they to be executed? Under present conditions, we could kill ten or twenty a day and still—

CAPTAIN   We do not work in any such haphazard fashion!

LIEUTENANT-COLONEL   [*turning his back on the captain and pointing in the direction of the shore*] Tell me, sir, what are your thoughts about the soldiers in the front lines? Has it ever occurred to you, Captain, sir, that there's a great deal of dissatisfaction among them? Why should civil administration be allowed to waste its time, when those men are down there on the beach, working day and night to build fortifications and keep the enemy from landing?

CAPTAIN   The responsibility for the work of the civil administration lies entirely with me, and I don't take orders from an army lieutenant-colonel.

LIEUTENANT-COLONEL   It seems to me, sir, that we in the army take our responsibilities differently than you do in the navy.

CAPTAIN   What!

LIEUTENANT-COLONEL   [*ignoring the captain*] You men are soldiers in the army, and as long as you are, you will take your responsibilities seriously, you hear? You're not going to sit around in the jungle and think you're getting away with something. I won't let you!

CAPTAIN   Every man here is working in the civil administration under my command.

LIEUTENANT-COLONEL [*ignoring the captain*] It's the army's job to beat back the enemy, you hear, and if you forget it, I'll drag you off to the front lines myself.

CAPTAIN Get out! Report to the general!

LIEUTENANT-COLONEL [*ignoring the captain*] Last fall and this spring, the enemy sent task forces out on reconnaissance missions to the island, but it's a different story now. Look at them! More than thirty ships, ready to invade this island! The slightest let-down on our part, and we're all blown to bits, you hear?

CAPTAIN Get out! Get out! Get out!

LIEUTENANT-COLONEL [*ignoring the captain*] Understand? The slightest let-down, and we're blown to bits! [*exits*]

CAPTAIN [*to Kanohara*] How is the investigation going?

KANOHARA Sir, may I speak frankly?

CAPTAIN What is it?

KANOHARA There might actually be spies here, sir, but I can't believe there could be any large-scale spy ring, the kind of thing the lieutenant-colonel is always talking about. I can't believe it, given the general level of the islanders' intelligence.

SERGEANT I think he's right, sir. Since he [*pointing at Kanohara*] joined the staff, he's been practically everywhere on the island. There isn't another Japanese soldier who has made as many friends among the islanders as he has. I've heard him say that many times, sir, and since I've started interrogating the islanders too, I've come to think he's right, sir.

CAPTAIN But you think it's possible that there are spies?

KANOHARA Yes sir, assuming that the enemy instructed the natives in spy work before they evacuated this island, and assuming that they left behind some five or six hundred rockets. However, sir, we haven't found even one burned-out rocket shell.

MAN A But one man did see a light in the sky. Supposing they tied the signal rockets they were going to fire to the top of a palm tree. We'd never find the shells, would we? These people are better than monkeys at climbing trees.

KANOHARA There hasn't been one instance where two or more people saw the same light from different places. Look at this list. On the second of this month, at twenty-three hundred hours forty minutes, Private Superior First-Class Tachikawa saw a red light rising at an angle of forty-five degrees for three seconds at the western extremity of the island. On the third, at zero hundred hours thirty minutes, a soldier from the garrison saw a white light rising at an angle of fifty-five degrees for two seconds at the northwest corner of the east airstrip. The same for every other case on this list, only one man in one place! Then look here. White light means a position left undefended by the Japanese; yellow light, a position suitable for landing. Surely these are nothing more than suppositions we made from looking at the list.

CAPTAIN   Yes, but there have to be spies.

KANOHARA   Sir?

CAPTAIN   And preferably a well-organized spy ring. Why, there must be one around, for all the reasons the lieutenant-colonel gave us just now. Well, carry on with the investigation as you see fit. [*exits*]

SERGEANT   Come on, let's get to work. With this many battleships around, it wouldn't make a bit of difference even if there were spies, but an order's an order. Remember, "To receive an order from a superior is to receive an order from His Majesty, the Emperor." [*to the civilian employee*] All right, come on, bring a suspect from the cave. [*to Man A*] Get out if you're not on this detail.

MAN A   Come on, give me a break. Let me help you a little. I'll get hell if I don't do something. There's nothing else to do around here anyway. Come on, I'll help you. [*Man A and the civilian employee exit.*]

The native boy enters.

KANOHARA   Hello! What's wrong? Dangerous here! You—run off—hide in shelter. You bring that for me? [*He takes a coconut from the boy and pats him on the head.*] Thank you very much. [*to the boy as he stares at the sea*] You can't do—can't stand here look at sea. Those ships—not toys. Okay, hurry back to the shelter now. [*The boy exits.*]

SERGEANT   Hey, are you sure you can speak his language, whatever you call it?

KANOHARA   It's a hobby of mine, learning foreign languages.

SERGEANT   Well, I guess if you don't learn it here, you won't
learn it anywhere. They sure won't be teaching that in
any school I ever heard of. You know, that kid really likes
you.

KANOHARA   That's how kids are, even if you don't know their
language. Besides, he reminds me a lot of my own boy.
[*He yells.*] Hey, come down tree. You can't climb tree look
at ships. Bad trouble! Very bad trouble! Good! You down!
[*to the sergeant*] These people are great at climbing trees.

SERGEANT   There they are, they've come back. All right, what
are the charges against the woman? [*He stands up holding
a pole. Man A and the civilian employee bring in Woman A, a
native.*]

KANOHARA   She's—

SERGEANT   What are the charges?

KANOHARA   Sir, she—she's the mother of the boy who was here
just now.

SERGEANT   What?   [*For a moment, he is surprised but then immediately
ignores Kanohara and turns to the civilian employee and Man A.*]
Come on, what are the charges?

CIVILIAN EMPLOYEE   They say that this was found in her house.

SERGEANT   What's this? It's just a lamp, isn't it? [*to Kanohara*]
Translate into that language, whatever it is.

KANOHARA   Yes sir.

SERGEANT   All right, ask her what this is. Come on, grab the pole
when you ask. You've got to impress them when you ask.
Impress them, got it?

KANOHARA   Yes sir. What is this?

WOMAN A   That's to make fire, at night.

KANOHARA   To make fire, at night?

SERGEANT   Hell, that sounds suspicious at me, to make fires at
night! [*He beats her buttocks with the pole and continues to do so
frequently throughout the scene.*]

KANOHARA   [*to the woman*] No, wrong! It make your house light
at night, no?

WOMAN A   It does.

KANOHARA [*to the sergeant*] Look, it's a lamp after all. That's what she says.

SERGEANT [*to the civilian employee*] Bring her husband here, too. It'd be quicker to question them together. They were taken together, weren't they?

CIVILIAN EMPLOYEE I'm sorry, sir, but I don't know which one he is.

KANOHARA Her husband is dead. [*to the woman*] Your husband was shot, no? He was, no?

Woman A nods and weeps.

SERGEANT Died? When?

KANOHARA When his house was being searched by some of our soldiers.

SERGEANT Were you there at the time?

KANOHARA No sir, I wasn't. I heard about it from the boy.

SERGEANT [*suspiciously*] Why was he shot?

KANOHARA The boy said he was shot because he tried to run when they came to search the house.

SERGEANT That sounds even more suspicious, doesn't it? Why'd he try to run away?

KANOHARA [*to the woman*] Husband run because he afraid, no? No? You too late to go away?

WOMAN A Yes. He ran because he was afraid.

KANOHARA [*to the sergeant*] She says he ran because he was afraid. That's all.

Man B and Man C suddenly appear.

MAN A Hey, what're you doing here?

MAN B So she's the spy! The bitch! [*He hits the woman.*]

MAN C She's a goddamn whore! [*He hits the woman.*]

KANOHARA What are you doing? Stop it! Stop it!

MAN A Hey, let me give you a hand. [*He hits the woman.*]

SERGEANT Hey, what the hell do you think you're doing? We're still on duty.

MAN B Yes, sir. We were just on our way to brigade headquarters, sir, and heard you were carrying out interrogation here. We came over to have a look.

SERGEANT   Fools! Say, now how'd he do it? [*He imitates the captain.*] Get out! Get out! Get out! Come on, get out, will you? This isn't a show. [*Man B and Man C leave. The sergeant and Man A light cigarettes.*] So now, she says her husband ran away because he was afraid? Now if that were true, wouldn't everyone whose house was being searched be shot trying to run away? Why didn't she run away?

KANOHARA   She says she was too late.

SERGEANT   [*to the civilian employee*] Come on, come on, what're you standing around here for. You got your duties. Carry them out!

MAN A   Hey, the lieutenant-colonel said to fry their nuts in oil if we had to, but she hasn't got any. Now what're we going to do? [*He suddenly burns her with the cigarette. She screams.*]

KANOHARA   Wait a minute, let me ask her some more questions. [*He strikes her with the pole.*] I'm going to ask you once more—

SERGEANT   Asking her more questions won't help, not with your broken language. [*to the civilian employee*] Pick up that pole and hit her hard, damn it!

MAN A   [*to the civilian employee*] The navy sure has made you soft. Here, let me show you how. [*He takes the pole and hits her.*]

SERGEANT   Okay! I'll stand on this side, you on that side, and we'll take turns hitting her. Don't skip a stroke.

KANOHARA   Sir, it isn't going to do any good to hit her. She still doesn't understand what's going on.

SERGEANT   Shut up! It's the Emperor's order. [*to Man A*] Ready?

MAN A   Ready! Set! [*He hits the woman, and as he hits her, he speaks to Kanohara.*] Come on, give a hand. Your duties don't end with interpreting, you know.

SERGEANT   It's taking us all this time because your interpreting is so lousy.

MAN A   [*letting up from hitting the woman*] All right, let's see who can hit her the hardest. Ready!

Kanohara, left with no more excuses, prepares to hit her with the pole but then hesitates. The woman suddenly gives a piercing scream and runs away.

SERGEANT   Hey, catch her! [*to Kanohara*] You son of a bitch! She got away because you were just standing there. Go and get her. [*to the civilian employee*] Go with him. Go on!

Kanohara and the civilian employee run off after her.

MAN A   [*offering a cigarette to the sergeant*] You know, this work is pretty hard.

SERGEANT   You fool! [*to himself*] Fool? This whole thing is stupid. I don't even know why I'm doing this anymore. In a few days the enemy will be here, and we'll all be dead anyway.

KIYOKO   Was that true?

MAN A   What? [*ambiguously*] Well, in a way.

KIYOKO   Then why were you able to come back?

MAN A   What?

KIYOKO   If it was the way you say it was, all the Japanese forces should have been destroyed a few days later.

MAN A   Oh, that? Well, the truth is that one morning, a few days later, the battleships suddenly weren't there anymore.

KIYOKO   How was that?

MAN A   I guess their strategy must have changed suddenly. They just all went away. What a bunch of fools we looked like. The only thing left was that island, and that began to look more brutal every day.

KIYOKO   More brutal?

MAN A   Sure. The order was out to get rid of the spy ring while we still had the chance, because the next time the enemy came, we really would all die. Frankly, though, the worst of the lot were the officers. Your husband and I—we didn't really do anything very much.

KIYOKO   Well, and did the enemy come and attack you again?

MAN A   No, the defeat came instead. Defeat, only a few days later.

KIYOKO   And nothing else had happened in the meantime?

MAN A   No, nothing else to speak of. Well, I suppose there was one thing. Sixty-six islanders were executed. That's all. And—two, I think—died during interrogation.

Woman A's piercing scream is heard in the distance.

SERGEANT   What was that?

MAN A   A woman screamed.

The civilian employee comes running back.

SERGEANT   What happened?

CIVILIAN EMPLOYEE   She suddenly climbed up to the top of a tall palm tree—

SERGEANT   She can't climb to heaven, can she?

MAN A   Is Kanohara keeping watch on her from below?

CIVILIAN EMPLOYEE   Then she threw herself off the tree.

MAN A   The woman? Threw herself off?

CIVILIAN EMPLOYEE   Yes.

SERGEANT   Well, anyway—I guess that's what they're good at, climbing trees. Not much we can do about it. [*to Man A, who is about to go and see*] Forget it. Leave them alone.

Presently Kanohara comes back, holding the boy in his arms.

MAN A   Hey, isn't that the kid who's always hanging around? What are you doing with him now?

Kanohara remains silent.

SERGEANT   Did he see what happened?

Kanohara still remains silent.

SERGEANT   Well, did he? Did he see his mother throw herself off from the tree?

MAN A   That was his mother?

KANOHARA   [*very precise enunciation*] Yes sir, he saw it. He watched her fall and die.

CIVILIAN EMPLOYEE   You mean, this kid was hers?

Kanohara, Kiyoko, and Tobosuke stare at the boy.

SERGEANT   What the hell! These people don't even know enough to cry when their parents die.

KANOHARA   [*a monologue, but as if spoken to the boy*] Still dazed? It was too sudden. Come on, let's go.

SERGEANT   What do you mean? Where are you taking him?

KANOHARA   To the shelter.

SERGEANT   Son of a bitch! We can't let him go.

KIYOKO   Why not?

SERGEANT   He can still talk, can't he, if he's alive, even if he is just a kid.

TOBOSUKE   What are you saying!

SERGEANT   We're in the civil administration. It's our duty. We have to keep order among the natives. Strangle him and bury him someplace with his mother.

KANOHARA   The child has nothing to do with this.

SERGEANT   You're the one who said he did. Didn't you just say he saw the whole thing?

KANOHARA   I'll talk to him later. He'll understand.

SERGEANT   And what the hell are you going to tell him? Come on, someone, hurry up, do it.

KANOHARA   No, I—

SERGEANT   You'll do it?

KANOHARA   I will not do it, never!

SERGEANT   What do you mean, you son of a bitch? Are you refusing to obey an order?

KANOHARA   I absolutely will not do it.

SERGEANT   You goddamn son of a bitch. Do you know what happens to people who refuse to obey the Emperor's orders? [*He strikes Kanohara down.*]

MAN A   Sir.

SERGEANT   What?

MAN A   Maybe he's right, sir. I mean, sir, after all, it's only a matter of days before the enemy lands.

SERGEANT   Shut up, will you! [*He slaps Man A. To the civilian employee*] And what the hell are you doing, just standing around there! [*He slaps him.*] You son of a bitch! You sons of bitches! Sons of bitches! Every single, last one of you, sons of bitches! [*He bursts out crying and continues to slap all three men wildly.*]

*   *   *

LIEUTENANT-COLONEL   The situation, sir, does not look very good. At present, we're simply stuck here in this P.O.W. camp, but it's clear that we'll soon be taken to prison as suspected war criminals and tried under martial law. The problem, sir, is how we can get through the trial alive. I've taken it on myself to talk with the officers from the legal staff and the civil administration and find out what I could from them. I'm telling you sir, during the war, the whole bunch of them used to walk around looking like they owned the place, but you should see them now. They're hopeless, but that's not the worst of it. They're all of them specialists in law, and not a single one knows anything about international law or military trials. Not a single thing! The only thing that seems certain is that business about the spies, you know—whether we went through with the formalities of court proceedings when we executed them. And it seems pretty clear that we're in trouble because we didn't. It also seems very clear, sir, that we're going to have to insist that we did hold a trial, or else we won't be able to avoid responsibility for it. However, I've been told that it didn't have to be a proper trial. We'll be okay if we say it was only a military tribunal. Every chance I've had, sir, I've talked to the men involved, and I've told them all to talk it over among themselves to make sure they all have the same story. I've come to report this to the general and to you, sir, and to ask the general for his compliance. Sir? General, sir?

CAPTAIN   There's a question of procedure here. You should have asked the general for his opinion before you did anything.

LIEUTENANT-COLONEL   But, sir, what has the chain of command got to do with anything now? At this point, to get things moving—

CAPTAIN   I disagree.

LIEUTENANT-COLONEL   —to get things moving is essential. The chain of command is not—

CAPTAIN   That's not what I'm talking about. I disagree with your silly opinion. As far as I'm concerned, we should go to the trial and tell them exactly what happened. We were in hostilities. It seems perfectly legitimate to me to execute a spy during hostilities without a trial.

LIEUTENANT-COLONEL   But that's exactly what the specialists are saying is not legal.

CAPTAIN   So what! What if it isn't legal? It's far too late for us to play this petty game and make a scene in the trial. We should simply go and stand in the courtroom and tell them exactly what we did.

LIEUTENANT-COLONEL   But a trial is a kind of battle, too, isn't it? I mean, as long as they plan strategy to attack us with, sir, wouldn't it be natural for us to do some planning of our own?

CAPTAIN   Why, you slimy son of a bitch, you still want to play staff officer? You're wasting your time. I'll never consent.

LIEUTENANT-COLONEL   I would like the general's opinion.

GENERAL   It finally boils down to who had the ultimate responsibility for all this. I did. Stop playing games.

LIEUTENANT-COLONEL   [*with a sneer*] You may, sir, indulge yourself with these visions of responsibility, but it won't work in court, particularly in a military tribunal. I assure you, sir, that I have not been talking about games at all. I'm talking about strategy, as I just explained. And you don't have to worry about responsibility, sir, because if we do it my way, the responsibility will go to the appropriate person. Is it agreed, then? [*to the Captain*] Is it agreed? All right, if we agree, then there are a few facts I want you to memorize concerning the particulars. The first is that we held three tribunals of our own, okay? I will now proceed with the particulars. First, the dates, then the weather on those days, the place, the shape of the tent, the proceedings of the trials, and the condition of the defendants. The real problem we're facing, however, is the amount of time the trials took. Remember, the natives witnessed everything we did, from the time we collected them in the tent to the time we dragged them off to the execution grounds, and if we divide the time up by the number of people we executed, that would give each defendant one or, at best, two minutes. That, believe me, is going to be a real problem, but there's nothing we can do about it. All right, then, here are the items in order. The first tribunal was held on July 29th of this year. July 29th at thirteen hundred hours. Got it? July 29th at thirteen hundred hours—

*   *   *

*A chorus of monkey-like chattering arises from the spectators,
who cannot be seen by the audience.*

PROSECUTOR   The defendants acted contrary to the laws of that
very humanity to which they belong; they transgressed
international law and custom; they violated the Articles of
War. Gentlemen of the Court, the events of this affair are
utterly transparent at every step; all the defendants are
guilty of these outrages, and as for the idea that some of the
defendants bear greater responsibility than others, I, the
prosecutor, for one—

A chorus of monkey-like chattering

PRESIDING JUDGE   [*hitting what serves as his table with a gavel*] As
witness for the defense, the former brigadier general is now
permitted to take the stand.

The general appears in the witness stand.

PRESIDING JUDGE   The defense is now permitted to begin direct
examination of the witness.
LAWYER   [*a Japanese—very timidly*] Since the defense has been
refused permission to call natives of the island to the stand
as witnesses, we have been forced to call upon the brigadier
general, who is himself a defendant, to take the stand as a
witness on our behalf.
GENERAL   That is not so. I have taken the stand on my own
initiative.
LAWYER   I see, sir. At any rate, then, though forced into the role
of witness, given your noble conception of responsibility,
which would have it that you alone bear sole responsibility
for—
PRESIDING JUDGE   The court cannot permit any such vague line
of questioning. Witness, do you or do you not regret the
fact that through the action of the units under your command, a large number of natives of this island were sub-
jected to wrongful interrogation, unfair trials, and then
summarily killed?

GENERAL   Wrongful interrogation? Unfair trials? Who other than God or I has the right to judge, to conclude that these were wrongful and unfair without precise investigation? Of course it is my responsibility that I have not investigated the actions of my brigade in such precise detail as the court would propose, but as long as I have not, I can answer neither yes nor no to the court's question. While I was still a prisoner of war, I had occasion to read the Bible, something which I had not done for a long time. I came across one passage which left a truly great impression on me: "Let him among you who is without sin cast the first stone."

PRESIDING JUDGE   We are not here to discuss the Bible! The prosecution has been seeking permission for cross-examination for some time now. The prosecution now has the floor.

PROSECUTOR   You previously stated that you opposed the execution of even a single person, but on this occasion you knew beforehand that a large number of islanders would be executed. How do you explain this?

GENERAL   I can only blame myself for this affair.

PROSECUTOR   Were you consciously aware at that time of the fact that you were acting in violation of the various customs and articles of warfare on land and at sea?

GENERAL   At that time I did not take those customs and articles into consideration. I remember having studied such laws and customs once, a long time ago, but on the occasion under question I could only pity those people who were to be executed.

PROSECUTOR   You were a brigadier general, the man in charge of the troops garrisoned on that island, and yet you still can say something as infantile as that in public without shame? You yourself have acknowledged that you made no attempt to do something which you, by your own admission, could have effected immediately if you had chosen to as commander of that island. The prosecution has verified that fact and rests its case. [*He immediately turns around. The figure of the general disappears, and now we find that of the navy captain facing the prosecutor.*] But were there any lawyers for the defense in this so-called spy trial? From your accounts I am to understand there were none.

CAPTAIN   I am afraid that my knowledge of the law is practically equivalent to zero.

PROSECUTOR   I am not asking about your knowledge of the law. I am only asking if there were any lawyers for the defense present or not.

LIEUTENANT-COLONEL   [*suddenly, from the side*] Am I correct in my understanding that the term "spy trial" was used just now?

PROSECUTOR   I said spy trial.

LIEUTENANT-COLONEL   But I would like the court to acknowledge that this was never a "spy trial" at all, but something of a lesser nature, merely a military tribunal convened to try spies. And it is my understanding that a military tribunal is ordinarily composed of several officers acting as judges and one officer acting as prosecutor. Therefore—

PRESIDING JUDGE   I do not need to hear a lecture about tribunals from you. Mr. Prosecutor, what do you think?

PROSECUTOR   Well, from what we've heard from the present witness and from those before him, we could possibly consider this to have been a military tribunal. Sir, what is your opinion?

PRESIDING JUDGE   Well, I'm inclined to agree with you, that a military tribunal was convened and sixty-six islanders were executed.

PROSECUTOR   Let's look at it this way, sir. Supposing a proper military tribunal had been convened, and as a result, and only as a result, of that, the islanders were executed. My concern for war criminals would then have to focus on those soldiers who carried out direct interrogation, on those soldiers who committed the tortures in the course of the interrogation and caused two natives to die at that time. I am concerned with the men who actually perpetrated the crime.

*   *   *

The Japanese lawyer, Man A, Man B, Man C, and Kanohara

LAWYER   You fellows keep accusing me of being powerless and incompetent, but you keep forgetting that I'm a prisoner

too. I'm not really a lawyer here. When the camp commander at the P.O.W. camp called me in, I just about flew
through the window; I was sure they had finally accused
me of war crimes too, you know. So then they told me I
was your lawyer in this case. So what's that supposed to
mean? I mean, they appointed me because I had been on
the legal staff, but—

MAN A   That means you're supposed to get out there and defend
us, like an officer of the legal staff should!

MAN B   Look, you didn't say a single word in our defense yesterday.

LAWYER   Sure, look, I know what you're saying, but what might
happen to me if I said something careless while I'm defending you? For all I know, they're just waiting for some
slip to trip me up on and make a war criminal out of me
too. That's—

MAN C   Listen, it's already settled that we're war criminals. We're,
we're—we're perpetrators, that's what. Perpetrators!

LAWYER   That's just it. If I became a war criminal, I wouldn't
be able to defend you any more, would I?

MAN A   What the hell! That would hardly be any different from
the defense we're getting now! Get the hell out there and
defend us, will you! You were a soldier in the Imperial
Army, weren't you?

KANOHARA   Look, we're wasting time. Let's talk about what we're
going to do.

LAWYER   Exactly. Only, remember, the most important thing for
me is to avoid making a bad impression with the judge and
the prosecutor. That's the only thing I'm worried about.

MAN B   But that doesn't mean you have to stand there like a deaf-
mute!

MAN C   Anyway, you're the only one who understands how a trial
is set up. They can't go around deciding we're perpetrators
just like that, can they?

LAWYER   That's the thing. We don't really know either. This
war trial, or whatever they're calling it—it's completely
different from any trial we've ever seen in Japan. Up to
now, we simply called the defendant into the court in the
name of the Emperor and informed him what he was guilty
of.

KANOHARA What do you want with us? You said you had something to arrange.

LAWYER Right. Now look, what they call a trial goes like this.
Both the prosecution and the defense call up witnesses,
and each side gets to question each other's witnesses. And
questioning can get pretty rough. After that, they bring the
trial to a conclusion. It's like a football game. The thing
is, for our side, for the defense, we can't find a single islander
who's willing to stand as our witness. I've been around to
each of the defendants to ask who knows someone, and we
can't find a single islander. Now I'm telling you, it's going
to work against us very badly if we don't find someone from
the islanders who will testify for the defense. I want to know
if you know anyone we can use.

MAN A You've got me. I don't know anyone. [to Kanohara] You
were the one who knew them the best, weren't you?

LAWYER That's what I hear. You had a number of friends among
them.

MAN B Sure he did. Isn't there someone?

MAN C Please, think of someone! Our lives are at stake, man.

Kanohara remains silent.

LAWYER I don't suppose I need to remind you, but most of the
defendants, big and small, are going to get it anyway, there
are so many. And we're doing a service if we help make
that number smaller, even by a little. I'm not talking to
you as a lawyer any more. I'm begging you as a Japanese.
Please, can't you think of someone?

Kanohara remains silent.

LAWYER Look, from the natives' point of view, they were doing
fine until we occupied their island. As far as they're concerned, we made a mess of the island. Besides, now, when
Japan has been defeated, they're hardly going to come
around to defend us if they have to defy the victors to do
it. It's only natural. But if we don't find at least one witness, I told you what would happen. It will really work
against us. Can't you think of someone?

Kanohara remains silent.

LAWYER   Besides—

KANOHARA   Wait a minute. I wonder. Tell me, what is it you want him to say—the witness, the native?

LAWYER   Well, for example—as an example—it would be hopeless to try and make one of those ignorant aborigines say something that made sense anyway, so—yes, of course— think of it the other way around! Since this trial has been set up to decide who the perpetrators were, have the witness point with his finger. It's the simplest example I can think of. Which of these Japanese tortured people? At least those who aren't pointed at would be helped.

KANOHARA   But if they're to point out which ones of us tortured them, surely the islanders will stand witness for us if we explain the situation to them.

LAWYER   Not at all. They won't take the stand for any reason whatsoever. That's what they're all saying, that they won't testify for the defendants, for the Japanese, for us! I don't know. Maybe it just shows how ignorant they are.

KANOHARA   I see. So all the adults have said this to you?

LAWYER   Adults?

KANOHARA   Yes, the native adults.

MAN A   [*to Kanohara*]   Say—

KANOHARA   Exactly. You think we should get the boy, do you? [*to the lawyer*] Can a young boy serve as witness? There's no age limit, is there?

LAWYER   Not at all. In this case, anyone will do, a child, even an idiot.

KANOHARA   If a child will do, there is one, a boy. He's still very young and doesn't understand things, but he knows enough to point if he's told to. I'm sure he could do that much.

MAN A   Hey, are you sure it's okay? The kid might remember what happened that time.

KANOHARA   [*smiling*]   You're the one who said to get him, aren't you?

MAN A   That's fine for you. He knows you. What about us?

KANOHARA   Don't worry. The one thing he won't do is point at you. He doesn't know you.

MAN A   No, that makes it all the more dangerous. It does, doesn't it? Hey, what's wrong with you?

TOBOSUKE   [*showing the pistol to Kanohara*]   Don't you need this anymore?

MAN A   Hey, what's wrong?

KANOHARA   —Nothing. I was just thinking about—guilt.

MAN A   Guilt?

KANOHARA   [*smiling*]   Have you forgotten? "Someone's going to die, and it's either me or you." "Left, right, step by step—it's a dangerous game we play."

MAN A   I remember. "Fall with a thump and you're off to hell."

KANOHARA   "Left, right, step by step—it's a dangerous game we play." You remember now, don't you? The words have finally become real. "Left, right, step by step—it's a dangerous game we play." You finally see, don't you? It's about your own life. You see that, don't you? [*He laughs.*]

*   *   *

A loud roar of many people laughing

PRESIDING JUDGE   [*hitting what serves as his table with a gavel*]   The spectators will please remember that the witnesses have been brought here from a small, isolated island and furthermore have been made to testify in this solemn court, surrounded by a great many people. This change has been for them both drastic and abrupt, and they are therefore naturally amazed and terrified. We must observe the confrontation as it develops between the witnesses and the defendants, these enemies of mankind, in strict silence.

PROSECUTOR   Will the next witness please take the stand. [*A man from among the islanders appears at the witness stand. On the other side are lined up Man A, Man B, Man C, the sergeant, the civilian employee, and Kanohara.*] We must identify the criminals who carried out direct interrogation and torture of your people and who murdered two of you.

LAWYER   Your Honor, the prosecution just now alleged that two people were killed, were murdered. The facts are that one of these two was an old man nearly eighty, already severely debilitated, who died a natural death after the interrogation, and the other was a woman who committed suicide by throwing herself from the top of a palm tree.

PROSECUTOR   Witness, answer the question honestly. We have inferred that three men were involved. Are any of the men who tortured your people and killed two of you present here among these six men?

LAWYER   The defense objects. No one was murdered.

PROSECUTOR   If you do not know their names, point with your finger.

Native Man A hesitates and then points at each man in the line, beginning with Man A.

PROSECUTOR   You have pointed at six persons. We want three or less among these six.

Native Man A again hesitates and then points uncertainly at three men.

PROSECUTOR   Once again.

Native Man A again hesitates and then points uncertainly at a different group of three men.
A loud roar of many people laughing is heard as Native Man A disappears.

PRESIDING JUDGE   [*hitting what serves as his table with a gavel*]   Next witness.

Native Woman B appears on the witness stand.

PROSECUTOR   Witness, answer honestly. Of these six men, which three did you know best? [*Woman B points at the civilian employee, the sergeant, and Kanohara. The prosecutor begins with Kanohara.*] Under what conditions did you know this man?

NATIVE WOMAN B   Always.

PROSECUTOR   Always?

NATIVE WOMAN B   We always saw him around. Everyone knew him.

PROSECUTOR   Well, then, what about these two?

NATIVE WOMAN B   I knew them both well.

PROSECUTOR   Under what conditions?

NATIVE WOMAN B   Night.

PROSECUTOR   Night? What night?

NATIVE WOMAN B   Every other night.

PROSECUTOR   Every other night? Well, under what conditions did you know them every other night?

NATIVE WOMAN B   [*pointing alternately*]   They made love with me every other night.

The loud roar of many people laughing is heard as Woman B disappears.

PRESIDING JUDGE   [*hitting what serves as his table with a gavel*] Next, the defense will summon its one witness.

LAWYER   The defense calls its one witness from among the island population to the stand. At this time I wish to impress upon the court that the defense has no intention of indulging itself in the false logic of attempting to defend the guilty. I am confident that the witness whom we now call to the stand is a person who can testify in a pure and unprejudiced spirit. Will the witness please take the stand. Please take the stand. [*The boy appears at the witness stand.*] Please answer honestly. Who among the men here committed atrocities against your people? Please answer honestly. If you don't know their names, please point with your finger.

KIYOKO   Stop! Don't do it!

TOBOSUKE   Point!

KIYOKO   You don't need to point! You don't need to say anything! You don't need to do anything at all!

TOBOSUKE   Point! Point right at him with your finger! Or say his name out loud!

The stage lights dim out instantaneously. Darkness.

End of Act III

Act IV

CHARACTERS

The boy (Kiyoko's son)
Tobosuke
Kiyoko
Man A
Man B
Man C
Kanohara

The boy is found on top of the slide, where he was at the end of Act II. He now slides down to the bottom. At the same time as he slides down, the stage lights are brought up full to present to us once again the original park.

BOY [*looking at the adults without moving from the bottom of the slide*] What's everyone doing? Let's go home, Mom, now!

MAN A [*after a brief pause*] It was a dream, a dream.

TOBOSUKE A dream?

MAN A That's the only way I can think of it now. It was all a bad, bad dream.

TOBOSUKE You must be joking. It was all a dream, you say? Let me ask you something. If a person is dreaming, sooner or later the time comes to wake up, doesn't it? But you still claim it's a dream when for you there's no awakening. Anyone who can live with a claim like that is lucky, isn't he? How about those of us who can't dismiss it as a dream? Tell me, what do you intend to do for us?

MAN A Do for you? What can we do? We don't have any more idea what we're doing here than you do. That trial was a mess, that's all.

TOBOSUKE [*imitating him*] The trial was a mess. Bravo, encore! That much we gathered from what you said. Oh, you'd better believe how well we know that. But there is something we don't understand. How can anyone who came back alive say it was such a mess and still be so complacent? If someone who had died told me that, I'd understand it all too well. But to be alive and to be so indifferent, to stand there so smugly! Doesn't that make you angry, Mrs. Kanohara? No, not angry. It simply is unconvincing. [*The boy by now has given up and goes off to the swing in the rear and begins to swing slowly.*]

KIYOKO In my husband's letter, the one he [*gestures at Man A*] brought back, do you know what he said? He found it very odd, he said, but he felt somehow at peace.

TOBOSUKE What did he mean?

KIYOKO I suppose he felt satisfied.

TOBOSUKE Satisfied?

KIYOKO After the trial—during that long, long wait until he

wrote the letter, I suppose—he found he could finally be convinced.

TOBOSUKE   How could he ever be convinced!

KIYOKO   Because a child who looked just like our boy pointed at him. [*All turn and look at the boy swinging on the swing.*] I suppose that's why he said what he did. "That is where guilt lies." That was what must finally have convinced him that guilt exists within himself as well. He finally came to accept that.

TOBOSUKE   [*after a brief pause*]   Mrs. Kanohara, are you convinced?

KIYOKO   [*angrily*]   Convinced or not! What difference would it make any more if I were? I would like to be persuaded, as he was. I want to accept it and forget it. More than anything else, I want to forget. To wish it away, to make it so that nothing had ever happened at all!

TOBOSUKE   I see. "I gave myself up to giving up hope, but now I'm given up to never giving it up completely." Is that it? What a put-on every intellectual is! What do you mean, conviction! And satisfaction! How can you have these when so much happened? Mrs. Kanohara, isn't it true that an awful lot of things happened?

KIYOKO   Yes, of course they did, and that's precisely why we've all gathered here to laugh and cry together. And yet, and yet, I still don't know.

MAN C   We were the bull's eye on the target. It was like a shooting gallery at a sideshow. The toy guns were badly made and wouldn't shoot straight, and whoever was unlucky enough to be hit was it, the guilty man.

TOBOSUKE   What difference does it make if the bullet is only cork when the person it hits dies anyway? Was that really what it was: the one who got hit lost, and the one who didn't won? I simply can't believe that's all there is to it.

MAN A   Remember the staff officer, the lieutenant-colonel? He came back alive. You can bet he's off somewhere, living a nice, quiet life.

TOBOSUKE   Don't play dumb. You know that swarms of people like that came back alive, and they're all clamoring to make swarms of children who look just like them. Oh, it's not just that, either: it's everything, you hear? If it all depended on the simple fact that the trial was a farce, who could make any sense out of it? Do you mean to say you're standing there with those silly expressions on your faces because it was a farce? Or that somebody was hanged just because it was a farce? Pull yourselves together! You didn't come here just to pay your respects to Mrs. Kanohara, did you? Not today!

MAN A   What do you mean?

TOBOSUKE   I've already told her everything. Everything from what I knew of him before he married her, from my feelings, to what I heard from you today, everything. That's where everything began today, there's no need to repeat it.

MAN B   What are you talking about? What did you hear from us today?

TOBOSUKE   Don't pretend you don't know! You know what you told him [*gestures at Man A*] earlier today, that her husband was executed!

MAN B   What?

MAN A   You fool! How could you—why, I never said—I'm sorry, Mrs. Kanohara, for some reason she must have thought that's what I said, but I never, never said anything like that.

TOBOSUKE   What?

MAN A   For some reason she must have misunderstood us completely.

TOBOSUKE   Misunderstood? You mean that was all a misunderstanding?

MAN A   What else could it be? I never said anything like that.

TOBOSUKE   You liar! Why, you told me so yourself! What a natural!

MAN B   I'm sorry, but I, at least, never, never said anything at all about his having been executed.

TOBOSUKE   What do you mean?

MAN A   That it was a misunderstanding on your part.

TOBOSUKE   [*breaks out laughing*]   Really? It was really a misunderstanding? You mean I assumed all this was true just because of some mistake on my part?

MAN A   Look, all I ever said—

TOBOSUKE   Mrs. Kanohara! Did you hear that? They say the whole business of your husband's execution—it's all nonsense.

MAN A   You're the one who thought we'd said that, not us. It's not our fault.

TOBOSUKE   Do you know what that means? That all this time I've been crying and carrying on over something that never happened at all. I've been putting on this show for no reason at all. Just because I jumped to conclusions! No, it was more than that. I had really convinced myself, I was serious! [*laughs*] I was utterly serious! The show of a lifetime, a performance never to be forgotten! [*Again she laughs.*]

pause

KIYOKO   He is dead.

ALL   What?

KIYOKO   He was hanged.

TOBOSUKE   He was?

MAN A   But how could he have been?

KIYOKO   I'm not lying. I was told so explicitly.

MAN A   But how could that be? Who told you?

KIYOKO   I went to the Repatriates Relief Bureau today. They told me.

pause

MAN A   [*to Man B*]   I thought you said you had stopped by the Bureau on your way here.

MAN B   Yes—well, that is, I talked with them for a bit.

MAN A   Talked? Where? Come on, didn't you say you were late getting here because you had stopped by the Bureau on the way? Mrs. Kanohara, is this certain? When did you go there?

KIYOKO   That's where I was when I went out just now.

MAN A   [*to Man B*]   What is this?

MAN B   Well—

MAN A   Well what? Did you stop by?

MAN B   Actually—

MAN A   What do you mean? Did you or did you not go to the Relief Bureau? Did you? [*Man B remains silent, and Man A suddenly slaps him.*]

KIYOKO   The official notification should come soon. What they told me was still unofficial.

MAN A   Forgive me for saying this, ma'am, but you're very calm, aren't you.

KIYOKO   [*angrily*] Calm? Who said anything about calm! I've simply spent a long, long time preparing myself, steeling myself for what would happen today. That's all. . . . Odd. I feel as if I've said that before. No, it's simply that I've said that to myself over and over again.

TOBOSUKE   [*after a brief pause*] Why didn't you say anything about his death before?

KIYOKO   You never let me say a word, did you? You kept on talking so fast I never had a chance to say anything before now. This is the first time you've let me say a word.

Tobosuke utters an exclamation of surprise, which Kiyoko covers with her next line.

KIYOKO   You yourself said that you were carrying on over something that never happened, that you were putting on a show for no reason. But think of it for a minute. If that's true in this case, how much more true it is for everything that happened. The whole affair, the entire chain of events began in something that never really happened, didn't it? You tortured and killed the people on that island because you thought the enemy was going to attack, and then they never did.

MAN A   But at that time everyone was convinced that they were going to. The only reason they didn't was because their strategy suddenly changed.

KIYOKO   That's not what I mean. Just when you thought the enemy was coming, the defeat came instead. It's the same as having been told a big lie, isn't it?

TOBOSUKE   A big lie? Who told it?

KIYOKO   God did, I'm sure.

TOBOSUKE   God?

KIYOKO   Who else could it be but God? That God you are so in-
tent upon defying.

TOBOSUKE   Yes, God.

KIYOKO   [*to the boy*] Let's go home. Grandmother's waiting all
alone. [*The boy does not hear and continues to play on the swing.*]

MAN A   Ma'am, when the official notification comes, of course
we'll want to pay our formal respects, but I wonder if we
might stop by your home now and offer some incense in
memory of your husband.

KIYOKO   You don't need to bother. But if you feel that strongly,
please make your offering in your own homes.

MAN A   What's wrong? I hope we didn't make you angry.

KIYOKO   No, I'm not angry at all. I just want to be left alone right
now. [*to no one in particular*] I've heard that men condemned
to death were left alone for the most part. They weren't
harassed very much in prison.

MAN C   Yes, that's true.

KIYOKO   Men condemned to death, particularly those condemned
by mistake, spent their days in good spirits. That's what
you said, wasn't it?

MAN B   Yes, they did. All the men I knew in that group were like
that. The meals we got were terrible, but for them each
meal seemed particularly good, they said.

KIYOKO   Every single, trivial thing must begin to look very important to such men, I suppose.

MAN A   But your husband kept up the fight as long as he could.
Even after his sentence was passed, he continued to raise
objections; not that the judge ever considered them.

MAN B   [*imitating the judge*] "In a military tribunal, defendants are
not permitted to make any statements once sentence has
been passed." That was the end of it.

MAN C   [*imitating the judge*] "However, the defense may, within
fourteen days from the present, submit an appeal for reduc-
tion of sentence, signed jointly by all the defendants, to the
regional commander." That was a mere formality. It wasn't
worth the paper it was written on.

MAN A   And yet he wouldn't give up. Your husband sent a long
letter in English to the regional commander.

KIYOKO   [*speaking to Tobosuke, unrelated to what Man A has said*]
I've heard a story about a soldier condemned to death
who said he was relieved, he no longer felt any pressure.
He didn't mean what he said to be particularly memo-
rable. For some reason he couldn't explain, he was happy.
The saddest thing he felt was parting with his friends. And
finally when he was being led off to the execution grounds,
as he crossed over a small river, they say he recited a poem
to the chaplain:
"Where
Does it flow to?
This tiny river"

TOBOSUKE   "Where
Does it flow to?
This tiny river" . . . No, no, it won't work, you can't
lure me on, too. And yet I admit, I understand your
desire to forget everything completely.

MAN A   You should, too. Everyone wants to forget, as quickly
as possible; even we want to. Only, the world won't let it
happen. Look at us. We served our ten-year sentence, so
they send us back from the islands to Sugamo Prison. Then,
pretty soon, they find it's too much trouble to take care of
trash like us, so they let us go, they spring us. What good
does that do? We're still branded as war criminals, and
nobody's about to forget it, either. Let me tell you, once
you're branded war criminal, everyone treats you suspiciously, like you really had done something.

TOBOSUKE   The world will forget. You don't need to worry, it
will forget right away. I'm telling you, by the time that
child is old enough to have a lover, how do you think it
will be? They will all have forgotten about who was a war
criminal and who wasn't. They'll drop you like some old
song. And I, the *manzai* comedienne, bear witness to it, so
rest assured, my friend, that's how the world is. Well, well,
so it seems that the curtain is about to go up on my show.

MAN A   Stop joking.

TOBOSUKE   Who's joking?

MAN A   You are, talking about curtains and shows. You're being inconsiderate.

TOBOSUKE   Who ever took me into consideration? And who ever asked them to? Don't be a fool. I kept a watch on them all the time to see just how much she really loved him. I mean, how else could I find out? After all, it's my principle never to interfere in other people's affairs. How else can we remain human? Why, even on that night, after we had said goodbye in front of his—in front of their house, I waited there in the shadows the whole night long. Their lights were on until morning, and then, finally, when morning came, I went home, you know. And ever since then, I've been thinking, thinking the whole time, making my preparations too, just like Mrs. Kanohara, wondering what I would do when the time finally comes. And now, today, this very instant, that time that has so worried me has finally come. Hasn't it? Hasn't that time come, now? It's come, I tell you, it's finally come. [*She begins to weep in long, deep sobs.*]

KIYOKO   For me, the curtain has fallen. [*to the boy*] Come, let's go home.

TOBOSUKE   Mrs. Kanohara, I've said all that I have to say. [*to the boy*] Your mother wants to go home. The show is over, folks, the exit's at the rear, thank you. [*to the boy, who is coming toward her*] Oh, I forgot. Won't you take my picture now? I'm not funny at all any more.

BOY   I can't. It's too dark.

TOBOSUKE   What? So it is. [*to no one in particular*] I guess that's how I am. I can't take a picture or have one taken of me. [*to the men*] Maybe so, but this much even I know. He took it upon himself to play a dangerous game. Left, right, step by step—it's a dangerous game we play. He didn't play it like some of the others did, trying to find a way out. He took it on and staked his very life on that game. He did it to protect what was most important to him. Do you understand? [*with great sincerity*] Well then, goodbye, everyone. [*She suddenly slaps Man A, Man B, and Man C.*]

All except Tobosuke exit.
The stage lights are brought down very low.

TOBOSUKE   Now I'm alone. I'm all alone. A beautiful sky—a

spray of stars across the purple twilight sky, was it? Oh, I'd forgotten. I still have this. [*She notices the pistol in her hand and aims it at something.*] Funny, the sight's blurred, a double-image. No matter how long I look, I can't bring your face into focus. [*She pulls the trigger. A roar. But she continues to speak, heedless of the roar, this time and all times after this.*] And yet, now that you're gone far beyond where I can reach you, I can talk with you as much as I want. I can, can't I?

KANOHARA   Pokey Tobosuke, still plodding along, but always looking for a stage, for a chance to sing your song. That's how you always were. Stay like that, don't ever change, you hear?

TOBOSUKE   [*laughs*] And you! You haven't changed either, always ready with a sermon the minute I say anything. Come here, closer to me. Remember? There used to be a board across here, we used it as a bench. The air raid—the incendiary bombs fell silently, the flames blazing up like jack-o-lanterns everywhere. [*Lights as from a huge conflagration illuminate the stage.*] Then, all of a sudden, you began to talk about a gravestone. You had already resolved yourself by then that you couldn't come back alive.

KANOHARA   I made it clear that I didn't want a funeral. I just wanted someone to put up a gravestone.

TOBOSUKE   And then you said that you didn't want a posthumous name carved on the stone, only your family name.

KANOHARA   You know the place on the side of the stone where the date of death is carved? I want the date and the place where I died in battle carved there.

TOBOSUKE   You didn't die in battle, you were hanged. Not even you ever imagined you would be hanged.

KANOHARA   Carve it there so that the world will always remember.

TOBOSUKE   I will never forget that you were hanged. Some people may want to forget everything completely, but I never will.

KANOHARA   Everyone wants to forget whatever was trying or unpleasant. Why else the saying that oblivion is the wisdom of the people?

TOBOSUKE   Isn't that why I told him not to worry about what people called him? Everyone in ten years' time will have forgotten who was a war criminal and who wasn't.

KANOHARA   But there's something else. Because people forget, evil will always be with us in this world. Take the men who acted so badly in this war. However bad they may have been, some of them are sure to be spared because of oblivion. They'll be spared and grow powerful once again, you watch. They'll be the prime ministers and corporation presidents. They'll start writing their outrageous statements again.

TOBOSUKE   Everything changes with the times, they say. [*She aims the pistol at something. A roar.*] I don't suppose you know this poem, do you?

> "After tomorrow,
> Who is there
> To fear?
> In the Buddha's lap
> I shall sleep peacefully"

It's well-known these days. The Chief of the General Staff wrote it as his last testament when he was condemned to death in the Tokyo Trials. I remembered it by chance when I heard that other poem just now:

> "Where
> Does it flow to?
> This tiny river"

Oh, these words are perfect for you, aren't they. Maybe you'll recite it when you die.

> "Where
> Does it flow to?
> This tiny river"

[*a roar*] How different human beings can be!

> "After tomorrow,
> Who is there
> To fear?
> In the Buddha's lap
> I shall sleep peacefully"

[*a roar*] What does it mean to be so shameless? It never even occurred to him to think about what he had done, or to wonder how what he did affected people like you and me.

You know, I've been thinking of using that poem on stage somehow, but I haven't dared to yet. I'm afraid there still are people who will get angry if I do. [*a roar*] Maybe ten or twenty years from now, when they've all forgotten, maybe then I'll yell down at them from the stage, "Have you all really forgotten so soon?" and tell them this story. [*a roar*] If, that is, I'm still alive and putting on a show at that time. [*a roar*]

KANOHARA   I don't want any eulogy carved on my gravestone. I'll be satisfied if people see it and realize that there once was a man who was hanged somewhere abroad and then think about him. As one of the characters in *Summer: A Romance of the South Seas.*

TOBOSUKE   I'm afraid there's only one place where we can raise that stone—in my heart. And I'm the one who can't take a picture or have it taken, either. [*She holds Kanohara in a motherly embrace. The stage lights dim. Unaware of Kanohara's exit, she is left alone on stage.*] Well, well, it's time for the show. The show is over, and yet, it seems the curtain is about to go up. [*exits*]

End